Copyright © 2010 by Robert Gest III

A Child's Eyes: Growing Up Poor and Black in the 1940's and 1950's

ISBN: 978-0-557-68533-2

A Child's Eyes: Growing Up Poor and Black in the '40s and '50s

By Robert Gest III

Introduction

Growing up in the segregated South posed many challenges, and in my early years I had to push against an array of obstacles. I had the advantage, though, of loving and caring parents, teachers and an entire community. A child's character is shaped by both positive and negative experiences, but the family, teachers and friends who guide a child through those experiences play an even bigger role, and it is these people who have made me the person I became. I have recounted many childhood incidents in mini-story form to create an earlier time period and paint with loving strokes the people who lived then in order to give young readers a perspective and feel for all that has come before them. Many of the stories are humorous, some sad, but all of them vividly portray my life as it was and what I did to get from there to here.

A Child's Eyes

My mother's life played like a variation of "Cinderella." My grandfather Horace Hall married Lula. I'm not sure what happened to my grandmother. She brought her three children into the household---Jesse, Evelyn and Willye. They joined my mother Luvenia and her sisters Esther, Mariah, Beatrice and Viola as well as her brothers Ernest and Robert.

My mother often had to stay home while her stepsisters went to school. Mama spoke longingly about not being able to get the education she wanted and she resented not being able to get a "proper education."

"Lula Hall's children could go to school but we could not. We had to stay home and clean and cook and wait on Lula Hall and her children hand and foot."

Front Row: Lula Hall and Horace Hall

Back Row: Willye, Evelyn and Viola

She used to talk about the whippings she got as a child. Grandpa Hall seemingly did pretty much what Lula Hall wanted done, and that included a healthy dose of discipline for mama and her siblings, but not for the stepsiblings. I imagine this may be where she came by her firm belief that one should not spare the rod for fear of spoiling the child.

I was sometimes the recipient of that philosophy when she would say, "Go out to that mulberry tree and cut me a switch – and if you know what's good for you, you'll bring a decent one. If you come back with one that's too small, I will go and cut one myself and I know you don't want me to do that."

After I came back with that switch (many times), she would sit her 300 pound plus frame in a straight-backed chair and invite me to place myself under the chair with my "hiney" sticking out. She would then proceed to "switch me" – stopping between whacks to admonish me for whatever it was I had done to dissatisfy her.

I was bold enough one day to plead with her, "Mama, please, go ahead and "whup" me and get it over with because you talking to me between licks is killing me"

Strangely, I never got the feeling that mama was being mean or vindictive. I always felt deep down that she was doing what she thought was best for me.

Yet, despite the fact that she wasn't formally educated beyond the fourth grade, she was my first teacher and she had plenty of knowledge to impart. In the early grades, she helped me with homework. She had practiced reading and writing and arithmetic on her own and became quite adept at all of them.

I know for sure that her love of education caused her to lecture me quite often about getting all the "learning" I could.

"Boy", she would say, "You can't ever get too much education and if you study hard you will not have to work as hard as your daddy has all his life doing backbreaking manual labor."

Her love for learning and her insistence that I be a good boy at all times, combined with her daily lectures, taught me to always strive to do the best I could in school. I always made good grades; mostly "A's" and ultimately graduated Number Two in my senior high school class.

In addition to book learning though, mama had other things going for her. In addition to having more common sense than Thomas Paine, she was a great cook, an even better seamstress and at times, it seemed as if she was also a doctor.

I think her cooking skills came in part from learning to cook a wide variety of food in ways that were both tasty and inexpensive.

She and daddy often told us kids about their walking five miles to a wild bean and pea field where the owner allowed poor folks to pick all they could carry.

She would look off into the distance and say, "We would start out early in the mornings, me and your daddy carrying burlap bags (they called them crocus sacks) over our shoulders. We walked that long and dusty five miles."

She would continue, "After we arrived at the fields, we would encounter many other poor black and white folks, hoping that the newly-grown beans had not been picked over too much. We would scavenge as best we could and often managed to fill up both bags and begin that even longer walk back home to Haines City."

They said they would have to stop many times mostly for the benefit of my mother because she said, "Those bags of beans were heavy."

It was clear to me that they persevered because they had a child to feed as well as themselves. Later on, in the 1940's, when my mother would make those wonderful green bean casseroles from store-bought beans, she would reminisce about the "Bad Old Days."

However, this was the 1940s when she was spinning her yarns. And, even though we lived in a small town, it was rural enough for us to keep chickens, hogs and other animals.

So, on many Saturdays, we would chase down one of the chickens and then my father would take the axe and cut off the chicken's head at the neck. The chicken would flop around, blood spewing from its neck like a veritable fountain.

My older sister Violet would then place the chicken in a container of very hot water and leave it there for a while. Anjo and I would then laboriously pluck the feathers from what was about to be dinner.

Of course Anjo always had something to say and most often it was, "I don't know why mama just don't go to town and buy chicken instead of making us get our hands all nasty and sticky."

But now, it was time for mama's magic.

She would clean the chicken--I will spare you the gory details-- and when the chicken was ready, she would heat a pot of Crisco lard and while that was melting, she would mix flour, pepper and salt to use as the batter. She then put the battered pieces of chicken in the boiling oil. And, when it was done, she'd put the pieces on a paper towel to soak up some of the grease.

That was the best chicken!

She often anchored our dinner with some delicacy she had "canned" the winter before. She called it canning but she had done what so many women of that era did, she preserved apples, grapes and other fruits in clear Mason Jars; the type with the clamp-on tops

Under her close supervision, I learned how to cook breakfast and even today, I am able to prepare some "mean" pancakes. I guess she felt that supper (dinner) was special so she did not insist that I learn to cook that meal.

Those Sunday dinners are still some of my fondest childhood memories. The Southern Fried Chicken, collard greens, baked sweet potatoes; washed down with Strawberry Kool-Aid. And, at the very end, some of her first-class Apple Pie.

In addition to cooking, mama excelled in the area of sewing. She made many of the dresses my sisters wore. To my great pleasure, girls' clothes were easier to make so she made very few items for me. Mama would often tell Anjo, "Girl, go get me that flour sack we emptied and washed last week."

Anjo would mutter under her breath, "Mama is gonna' make me another one of those print dresses out of those durned flour sacks. I hate to wear those things to school because the other girls point at me and laugh."

Mama bought McCall dress patterns and used emptied and washed 25 pound flour sacks which had print patterns suitable for clothing. After Mama had the pieces cut out according to the pattern, she'd roll out her trusty old pedal-driven Singer Sewing Machine and go to work.

My sisters were often ashamed and embarrassed by their dresses but they were clean and, some thought, quite attractive. Many years later I convinced mama to allow me to buy her a new electric Singer, but after trying it two or three times, she made me return it to the store and she continued using her very old but well known pedal-driven Singer.

Thank goodness, she never tried to make shirts for me.

As for her doctoring skills, we were never treated by medical doctors unless it was a very serious situation. These were the days when doctors made house calls. Mama needed no college-educated doctor. She had more what she called "home remedies "than Rockefeller had twenty dollar bills."

Mama would often go into the woods to find specific leaves and branches. She cooked them until they generated medicinal potions. When we had chest colds, she would place a foul poultice on our chests at night. It was made of lard and some other things that made it smell awful.

Amazingly, it cleared up the congestion in our chests.

Once I cut my wrist while playing with my homemade semi-truck and trailer. I had taken three blocks of wood and nailed the smallest block on top of the second longest block to form the truck's cab. Then, I got some empty thread spools and wire to make axles and wheels for my truck. I used staples to fasten the axles with wheels on the ends to the bottoms of both the truck's cab and the longer piece that was the trailer. Finally, I finished cutting off the top of an empty can and nailed that to the front end of the trailer that I somehow connected between the cab and the trailer.

One day I managed to get my wrist too close to the front of the trailer, the sharp can top, and cut my wrist.

Mama didn't get excited.

She said, "Boy, go get me a spider web." When I came back, she swabbed off the blood and applied the web from the now homeless spider to the cut. The blood coagulated and the web held the cut together. In a few days, I was ready for the next mishap.

When I got a sore throat, she would take a pencil, put cotton on the end, and dip the cotton end into iodine or mercurochrome. Then she would call me over, "Boy, open your mouth wide and hold your head back."

She would then stick that cotton covered pencil end down into my mouth, swab my tonsils with it and tell me to go somewhere and play. Yes, the sore throat that she had diagnosed as tonsillitis would disappear in a day or so.

Since the switches were a constant in my life, I sure was hoping that the teachers did not use switches on the kids in school.

I began school earlier than I am sure anyone planned.

My mother, who drove what passed for a school bus (our family car) also worked in the small school cafeteria. While mama worked, I ran wild around the school grounds, including sometimes into the one room school house.

One day, Mrs. Lucille James, the teacher for grades one through six said to mama, "Luvenia, why don't you buy that boy of yours a pencil and a tablet and send him to my first grade class. He is always in and out of there anyway so let's give him something useful to do."

I suppose I was a little anxious because I was about to do something new but I do not recall being scared. After all, my two sisters were going to the same school and I had never heard them say anything that would frighten me. I was excited though because from the very first moment I heard my sisters talk about school, I remember thinking, "I can't wait until I too can learn to read about Dick and Jane and Spot too."

I did really well in the first grade and at the end of the year, was promoted to third grade.

At the end of the school year, Mrs. James smilingly said to mama, "That boy of yours knows as much as the children I am promoting to third grade so if you have no objections, I am going to put him in third also."

Mama, bursting with pride, said, "No Mrs. James, I trust you to do what is best for him."

So there I was in third grade at age six.

One of my most vivid memories of that period has to do with the pencil and notebook in first grade. The pencil was eight inches long, about as big around as mama's index finger and as yellow as the sun on a bright cheery day. The tablet was nine inches wide and seven inches long with dull blue lines horizontally across its pages.

The size of the notebook was not its most striking feature. The thing that made this notebook stand out was the texture of its pages. The pages were coarse and grayish but most of all, the coarseness was magnified by what looked like little wood chips embedded in the paper.

I remember asking, "Mama, "Why does this tablet have pages that have wood chips in them and why is this pencil so big"?

I don't remember her answer but it was years later when listening to one of Bill Cosby's monologues that I understood that there were many other kids of my generation who had been blessed with that type writing equipment. No matter, when I was in school or doing my homework, I hefted my pencil and attacked my wide-lined tablet with glee, despite how difficult it was to work with it

Thus, it was Mrs. Lucille James, my teacher through the first few years of my life, who also instilled in me a love for school and education. She was a great teacher but more than that, she and her husband lived in Orlando, Florida; the big city. We would occasionally go visit them when we went to Orlando on the weekends and boy, their house was nice.

On one of these visits, I told Mrs. James, "One of these days, I hope I can live in a house as nice as yours."

I never forgot the shiny furniture or the tall mahogany china closet with all those figurines lined up inside like soldiers on the march.

As the years passed, I breezed through school, finding each day of learning a day for rejoicing,

There were only two blips.

When I was in ninth grade and just beginning to enter puberty, the Industrial Arts teacher asked me to go get a wheelbarrow.

With all the impudence of an acne-ridden, skinny kid of twelve, I told him, "If you want the wheelbarrow, you'd better go get it yourself."

That earned me an "F," and that solitary "F" cost me the number one spot in our graduating class. If not for that one "F", I probably would have been the class valedictorian. As it happened, I had to settle for salutatorian because Martha Taylor, who never told a teacher to get his own wheelbarrow, took the highest honor.

In addition to my school experiences, I lived through other events that were instrumental in making me the person I became.

I grew up in my rigidly segregated community with the belief that most, if not all, white people were really devils. My father was required to go to the back door of white people's houses. If he had even tried to approach the front door, he would have been lectured or "talked to" about "his real place in life." When a black person did something as bold as approach the front door of a white person's house, it was not uncommon for word to get around that so-and-so had gotten too big for his britches and must be taught a lesson. That is when, sometimes, the dreaded Night Riders would pay the black person a visit, often in the dead of night.

A personal experience I will never forget happened one day when I had ridden my bicycle to the nearby orange groves to help my father pick fruit.

Standing on the sidewalk, I heard an influential white man who was the owner of the grove, tell his twin three year olds, "Y'all see that truck full of people there. Anytime you see people who look like that, call them 'nigger.'"Now, you can call "Pap" Daniels by his name, Pap."

Pap was the nickname of this man who had worked for the white man for decades.

I also recall a never-to-be-forgotten trip downtown. We lived on the other side of the railroad tracks. We actually lived right next to the tracks. Therefore, when we walked to town, we most often walked the tracks because they led directly to town.

I did not walk to town often, especially not by myself, but when I was thirteen I tried it. On my way back home I was accosted by three white boys who looked to be about my age. They began taunting me, "Hey nigger; hey coon."

I was confident in my running ability so I hollered back, "Who you calling a nigger, you poor white trash."

Then I took off running as fast as I could.

They chased me but soon gave up because I was way ahead of them and putting more distance between us as we ran.

I suffered my second comeuppance when I arrived at Livingstone College in 1958 and tested into remedial English. Me, a Salutatorian, and I was in remedial English! The thing was, I had never heard of a gerund or a noun appositive. Of course, there is no way to know there are gaps in your education until you find yourself taking college tests and realizing that there is a world of "stuff" out there you know nothing about.

At Livingstone College, I had another turning point in my life. I learned that an important aspect of education should be learning to think for oneself.

When I studied sociology with the brilliant young Dr. Stanley Smith, he opened my mind and made me realize that we are all products of our society; our church, our home, our school. Folks could not be blamed entirely for who they were and what they thought. They were simply living out the life they had been taught. They most often did not think about it; they just did what they did. And, if they didn't experience something different, there was no reason for them to change.

Because of this and other experiences in my adult life, I was disabused of the notion that any group of people is inherently evil. Education, school and adult experiences, like travel, changed my world views.

As I enter the twilight of my life, I look back and see that my life is different than I imagined, but I know that it's not only my parents and many teachers who are responsible. I have to take some credit too!

Long ago, I concluded that life could be largely unfair. It seems that those who have keep on getting, and those who have not, keep on not getting. Nevertheless, I realized that with a little education, a bit of luck and a lot of perseverance, it is possible to change things. I have achieved far more than I thought possible.

And when it sometimes seemed impossible, I remembered what my daddy used to say.

"It could always be worse"

But it can be a lot better too!

I dreamed of being in the U.S. Air Force and flying through the wild blue yonder, but the dream was just that – a dream. I knew of no other black Air Force officers, although there were some. I knew of no other black Air Force pilots though there were some. Yet, I had this dream.

Thanks to my parents, Mrs. Lucille James plus other teachers, I reached for the moon. I understand that if one aims for the moon but falls a bit short, he is still among the stars.

This child has had plenty of stars in his life but the greatest star of all was his mother. She was not only his first teacher but also one of the most resourceful people he has ever known!

I've Learned The Most About Love

My mother frowned at me and said, "What's that in your mouth?"

Although I was almost 46 years old, I stammered much like a four year old. Why? I am sure it was because I was visiting my parent's home in Haines City, Florida.

I had forgotten where I was. And, horror of horrors, I had unthinkingly fired up a big green smelly unhealthy cigar. I hadn't thought about how my mother had always complained about my father's pipe and cigars and her constant concern about my health.

I told her it was only a cigar.

"It is a cigar. I can see that. Put it out."

Once again, without thinking about who and where I was, and emboldened by my status in life as a responsible, professional adult who was a Colonel in the United States Air Force, I said, "But ma, I'm 45 years old, a full grown man.".

"I don't care how old you are, you're not smoking in my house so put that thing out."

As one who grew up in the "olden days, I did as I was told. I put it out.

I thought back to all the times when the love my mother had for me was evident.

One day I came running home spitting red and crying like there was no tomorrow.

"Mama, mama, I am bleeding from the mouth. I must be bleeding to death and I am not ready to die!"

Perhaps some might think I was being a bit melodramatic at a mere eleven years old, but I had not come to the teen years when we think we are invincible and invulnerable.

Mama was the doctor, the cook, the disciplinarian and any other role that was needed. Anyway, she dropped everything she was doing and ran to me, almost as hysterical as I was.

"Somebody, anybody, call an ambulance. Oh, God, somebody take my boy to the doctor."

She was going to pieces!

Mrs. Ruby Davis, the neighbor from up the street, was visiting.

She said, "Come here boy and open your mouth."

I did. She looked inside and told me to spit.

After I spit, she told me to spit again.

Mrs. Ruby noted that the spit was getting a lighter red each time, so she asked me just what I had been doing.

"Playing with the other boys and going to Mr. Ben's Drug Store to buy candy and I was eating it on the way home when I saw I was bleeding."

"What kind of candy were you eating?"

"Red Hots."

Mrs. Ruby turned to my distraught mother and said, "There ain't nothing wrong with this boy. He ate that darned candy and the color from the candy turned his saliva red."

My mother didn't know whether to hug and kiss me or beat me within an inch of my life. Fortunately, I got the hug all the while remonstrating me about scaring her half to death.

I also have vivid memories of the day I left for college. As a small town boy who had never taken a trip without at least one of my parents, I was about to head off to Salisbury, North Carolina. My mother and father took me to the Greyhound Bus Station for that 22-hour bus ride. I boarded with all the cockiness a seventeen- year-old can muster and took my seat about halfway down the bus, at a window where I could see and hear my parents.

My mother began to cry. My father tried to console her by saying, "Luvenia, you know the boy needs to go off and get all the schooling he can so his life can be better than ours has been."

He couldn't calm her.

My always soft- spoken daddy later told me that for weeks my mother had tried to prepare herself for my leaving home. She never did quiet down and when the bus pulled off, she was still crying and waving, crying and waving.

Daddy, Robert "Bully" Gest and Mama, Luvenia Gest, circa 1962

I always knew that my mother loved me unconditionally. Even now up there in Heaven she is probably looking down on me, with approval sometimes and probably at other times wishing I would behave differently.

She was always hard on my behavior but soft on me as a person, expecting a lot from me. But she was always there when I needed her. Because of her example, I think I too am able to love unconditionally and I try to prove it by the way I live my life.

Daddy Beating the Odds

Heroes aren't always strangers you read about in comics and newspapers or see on the news and in movies. Some are people you know. Some even live with you.

My hero was my father.

He was one of three children and they all had to work, so they couldn't always go to school.

Daddy often said, "I went to school one day and that was in place of one of my brothers or sisters."

This is not so amazing when one considers that he was born in 1893, poor, black and the grandson of slaves.

Daddy often told us stories about his rough and tumble life as a young man.

"Boy," he would say, "I chewed tobacco and drank moonshine when I was too small to hide the bottle under my coat.

He told us there were many nights when he felt safer going to sleep with a pistol under his pillow. When he was twenty-nine, he was forced to leave his hometown in Summerton, South Carolina.

He said, "The white man who had made my wife pregnant told me that I had two choices: One, to stay there complaining and be lynched; or two, leave town and never come back."

I only knew this much because I overheard him and my mother talking one day about the girl who was born of this illicit union. Daddy was always a responsible person but he rarely talked about the girl because the memory was so painful.

Until later years.

After I was grown he talked more about this part of his life and made sure we children knew that in addition to our half-sister, Lue Tisher and half-brother, John, there was another child he claimed but was not sired by him.

We had always known about Tisher and John but not about Clammia, who by this time was living in Brooklyn, New York.

When daddy left Summerton, South Carolina he was thirty-four years old. I do not know how old his wife, Silla, was nor how long they had been married. I do know that after he left home, he had no further contact with Silla except through his brother, Felix.

Uncle Felix, who owned and operated his own farm, still lived in their hometown.

During the 1920's my father knew he would be risking his life and perhaps his wife's, so it was best that he did not try to contact her. I don't know if his wife was voluntarily with this white man, but it wouldn't have mattered, because during this period in the Deep South, blacks literally had no rights and no access to legal remedies.

Daddy was a realist; quiet and unassuming. Sometimes the veins would stand out in his neck like ropes of steel when he talked about having to leave his home, but he never raised his voice or showed the terrible pain he must have felt. He could "read the handwriting on the wall." so he left home and relocated to Haines City, Florida where he began the work he would do all his life---picking fruit, plus pruning and caring for citrus trees.

It was here that he met mama and married her in 1927 when he was thirty-four and she was seventeen. Shortly after their marriage, they moved to Vineland, Florida where the family lived until 1944.

He always told us he had divorced Silla and she had moved to Brooklyn to be near her three children; John, Lue Tisher and Clammia. However, many years later when considering social security benefits for my mother, they discovered that there was no record of divorce.

Mama said, "Bully, why don't you call up there and see if she will give you a divorce. I know it's been a long time and maybe she doesn't hold a grudge against you."

Daddy, who rarely talked on the phone, agreed to place this call. To his surprise and pleasure, Silla agreed to sign divorce papers. The very next day daddy saw a lawyer who drew up the papers and mailed them to Brooklyn.

A month later, daddy was finally divorced.

We teased daddy many times about his committing bigamy and marrying our mother under false pretenses.

He would say, "You children leave me alone and go find something to do."

His "something to do" was often to sit quietly while mama, who had only a fourth grade education, taught him the alphabet and how to write his name.

It was painful to watch.

It bothered me to see him, a grown, hard-working man, struggle to form letters with that pencil and paper. The love always shined in mama's eyes when she worked like this with daddy and I suppose this was my first exposure to what real love is and can be.

I am sure that because my father could not read or write, it became important to him that I get an education

Sometimes he would look off in the distance and say, "I could have done so much more had I gotten just a little bit of education. You children already know I helped build Highway US 301 from North to South. Well, they told me they wanted me to be an apprentice surveyor." Then he would look down, with the saddest of Beagle eyes and say, "I lost that chance to be somebody because I didn't know how to read or write. "

He would reminisce about other chances to "be somebody," but the one that seemed to bother him most was losing the surveyor opportunity.

One way my father compensated for his lack of education was with the book of multiplication tables he took with him to work. When he picked oranges, grapefruit or tangerines, he could look at the tables and figure out how much he had earned based on the number of boxes times what the organization was paying per box.

My father also talked about the times he cut down trees in the swampy lands of South Florida, often working hip deep in water infested with alligators.

Once, he reared back, laughed heartily and said, "A couple of times, old man 'gator got too close so I left the job as fast as I could. I knew how much damage that old alligator could do with that mean tail of his and I did not want to be anywhere close if he decided to whip it around."

We kids would urge him to tell us more about the alligators, but he would quickly return to his own private memories and change the subject.

He told me about the days when the sun was so hot outside he could smell his shirt burning on his back. I vividly remember his coming home barely able to move. When he worked in the hot Florida sun, the sweat would pour down his body and turn into salt. But, since he had to keep on picking, the salt would chafe and abrade his skin. At night, mama would cool him off with wet cloths and rub him down with Vaseline.

Life was surely not easy for my father.

There were also times when he was taken advantage of because of his innocence, naiveté or ignorance.

Once, he became indebted to a local loan company for $500 at a very high interest rate. His granddaughter Lynette wanted to enroll in a stewardess training program and because he wanted to help, and without checking with me, he went to the local loan company

Mr. Winger, owner of Haines City Finance Company, made loans mostly to poor blacks and whites who had no place else to turn. The interest rate on Daddy's loan was twenty-two percent! Daddy couldn't read the contract so it didn't matter if the interest rate was spelled out or if it was in the fine print. Daddy trusted this man to treat him right.

When it seemed as if he would never get the loan paid off, mama wrote and told me about it. I came home, went to the loan office, talked to Mr. Winger and looked at the contract.

I was livid.

The interest rate was compounding at a rate of ten percent a month on the unpaid balance. Daddy had been paying on the loan for over a year and still owed $490.

I thanked Mr. Winger for showing me the contract.

I went to my bank the next day, withdrew the unpaid balance and paid the loan off without comment.

Since daddy never earned more than $50 per week, he likely never would have been able to pay off that loan.

However, despite the low wages, he was able, with my mother's help staying home to raise us, to keep us in clean clothes and make sure we had food to eat. We didn't go hungry, although what we ate would be called cholesterol-laden meals today! I grew up eating pork n' beans, Spam, a lot of rice and homemade bread. My mother used neck bones, spareribs (which at that time were not considered a delicacy or a grilling meat) and the collard greens that she grew in the back yard.

Truthfully, I never knew we were poor until many years later. Moreover, despite all the woes and worries, my father always made me feel safe.

I still remember the time I saw a snake. I was four years old, sitting in the grass of the front yard of our home. The snake was jet black and maybe four feet long. He certainly looked menacing to a four-year old. I had no idea if the snake was friendly or poisonous. I only knew that it was a snake and snakes were bad.

Snakes could kill you.

I screamed and said, "Snake! Snake! Daddy, come quick."

My father, a slight but manly man, came running with the garden hoe and quickly dispatched the snake to "snake heaven."

Daddy was always soft-spoken and disciplined us with a stern look or the power of his presence. We listened, but we weren't afraid of him.

He taught us that work is honorable; that harsh words were not the answer. He took care of us no matter how hard the job was or how stifling hot the weather got. He made me realize there could be a better life for me through education.

A hero is someone who perseveres, overcoming great odds. He is a person who accepts his responsibility to take care of his family the best way he can.

Who knows how much more my dad could have accomplished with just a little bit of education?

What I do know is that no matter what, he loved us and he never let us down.

The First Christmas I Remember

I was five- years-old in 1942. Since it was the second year of World War II, we occasionally had "blackouts" with air raid sirens blasting. It sounded like the fire trucks or police were coming.

Fire meant someone was losing their home and police meant trouble with "the law," so the screech of the sirens was terrifying.

My bossy nine-year-old sister Anjo would say, "All right Violet and Flib, where are you going this time?"

My oldest sister Violet, who was thirteen and very quiet, said, "I'm going wherever mama and daddy go."

I thought it was fun scrambling around to hide in what I felt was the safest place---- under the big double bed where my mother and father slept.

The air raid on this particular night was two weeks before Christmas. I wedged myself under my "safe spot" and was surprised to discover a metal globe of the world under there with me.

I was accustomed to finding only dust bunnies under that gigantic bed!

The three of us didn't often question our mother because her "word" was the same as the law. We did feel free to ask mama questions about things we didn't understand, but it was too close to Christmas for me to risk asking about something that was obviously hidden.

I couldn't help wondering what it was doing there. However, I said nothing about my discovery.

Then, about a week before Christmas, as was customary, my father and I went to the woods in search of our Christmas tree. Daddy and I must have walked twenty minutes before finding the perfect pine, standing amidst many larger trees and seemingly just waiting for us to come and give it a new purpose.

Back home, Daddy said, "Boy, get some of those boards from the shed so we can make a footing for the tree."

Daddy cut two one by four pieces and said, "You hold the tree steady while I nail these two pieces on the bottom."

After we were sure the tree could stand upright and straight, we set it up in the house. Immediately, the living room smelled "piney" and life-giving, like the forest from which it had been uprooted.

Mama said to Violet and Anjo, "You two hang the silvery tinsel on the lower branches and I will take care of the higher ones."

Anjo, taller than Violet even though she was younger, said, "Mama, let's me and you put the bulbs on because Violet will just mess it up."

Violet, always quiet, did not say anything.

The three of them worked for a half hour hanging the tinsel and bright red, blue and clear triangle-shaped bulbs until our annual Christmas tree stood majestically in its own corner of the living room. It was beautiful!

I must confess, though, that I wasn't thinking so much about the birth of Jesus as I was about the much-anticipated gifts Santa would leave beneath our tree Christmas Day.

A week later, Violet, Anjo and I were up early. We had slept fitfully the night before, but now it was Christmas morning and not one of us bothered to wake our parents as we rushed to find out what Santa had brought us.

It was chaos as we tore through the small pile of Christmas wrapped presents. I said, pointing to a spot on my left, "When you find something for me, put it over there."

They each chose their spots as well.

After we had made three piles, we began opening our presents, ripping off colorful bows that only mama could make. I was overjoyed to see a cowboy pistol.

Because of the war, things like rubber and aluminum were rationed or scarce because they were used to provide the ships, guns and other things needed by the military. So my long-awaited pistol was made of something that looked like compacted tarpaper. It was solid and heavy and had no moving parts. Still, it was shaped like a pistol and I could not wait to run around playing cowboys and Indians.

For months, I had been racing around our house shooting at imaginary bad guys with a three-inch stick. Now I could properly engage the enemy with a suitable weapon.

In the meantime, Violet was teasing Anjo and said, "Goody-goody, it looks like you did not get that special make-up kit."

I paid little attention to them as I opened my second gift, the store-bought" dump truck I had admired in the toy store in Orlando. I had been making my own toy truck bed and cab for two years out of scrap wood, wheels from sewing thread spools and axles fashioned from stiff wire. So as much as I loved this store bought truck, I decided to play with my beloved blue and white brand new truck later so I could get to my last gift.

I gingerly opened the box and lo and behold, it was the globe I had seen under my parents' bed two weeks earlier.

I said nothing to my mother about seeing this under the bed, but I was confused, though not for long since I couldn't wait to play with my truck and gun.

Three years later, when other kids began to swear that there was no Santa, I remembered that Christmas and deliberately set out to find the truth by searching for hidden gifts in my Haines City house.

It was my misfortune that a week before Christmas, my mother caught me standing on a chair, looking on the top shelf in her bedroom closet with my hand on my present for that year.

She admonished me with a few well-chosen, never-to-be-forgotten words of disapproval.

She sat me down and said, "So since you are snooping around in my closet, how about telling me what you were looking for?"

Rarely did I lie to mama, so after stammering a few words of nonsense, I said, "I was trying to get an early look at my Christmas present.

She said, "Well, did you find one?"

"I think so but I guess you caught me before I could be sure."

Much to my dismay, she said, "Well, boy, Santa will never come to visit you again. Whatever you get for Christmas will be what your daddy and I are able to buy for you."

How I regret searching the shelves for the truth about Santa because at age eight, I lost the innocence, mystery and fantasy.

The Globe of the World meant so much more to me when I thought it came from the North Pole on Santa's sleigh.

Christmas would never be the same again.

Down The Street

One of my favorite family stories had to do with my father's penchant on Friday and Saturday evenings for going "down the street," or as folks would probably say now, "on the block." My mother told this story usually when she wanted to embarrass Daddy or if something reminded her of the event. I might add that it seems to us males that the female species never seems to forget anything that puts us guys on the spot.

On Friday evening, Daddy bathed, dressed and came into the living room to say he was "going down the street."

This was the first week they were married.

Mama says she told Daddy, "Wait until I change clothes because I am going with you." One must remember that this was 1929 when words and ideas like feminism and equal women's rights didn't exist.

Daddy, being the Alpha Male, said, "Luvenia, you are not going with me."

Mama, all of 17, years faced down Daddy who at the time was 34 years old.

She said, "Oh, yes I am."

Daddy started walking toward the front door to leave and Mama, having decided to go without changing clothes, ran around him and to the front door. Daddy stepped around her. Then, she says she made a critical error.

She swung at him.

He caught her hand in midair and said, "Now Luvenia, go somewhere and sit down." She said she was not about to back down and walked up to him, very close, face-to-face.

By this time in the telling, we kids were howling with laughter.

Mama continued the tale.

"Bully (my Daddy's nickname) didn't say another word. He put his hand in the middle of my chest and pushed real hard. I landed on my backside, slid all the way across the linoleum floor, and ended up with my back against the living room wall." Mama said Daddy calmly walked out of the door and went "down the street" where he stayed a few hours, returned home and acted as if nothing had happened.

Mama said although she was not hurt at all, she cried a little after he had left but then got over it. She would always end the story with the following words which would bring smiles all around, especially from Daddy. "And, I never again tried to follow him – 'down the street'."

Mama Got Left Behind

In my early years we lived on an orange grove – sort of like a plantation – in Vineland, Florida. Most folks referred to where we lived as Dr. Smith, Florida because he owned all the citrus groves in the area.

Every Saturday afternoon after my father got off work, we all would pile into our tan 1934 Chevrolet and head for Orlando to do our shopping. We would buy groceries for the coming week and anything else we needed that we could afford. I have fond memories of being carried on my father's shoulders to the various places. Sometimes we'd eat ice cream cones, popcorn and other goodies. Daddy would often buy some whiskey and tobacco because he would take a drink or two or three on the weekends and he regularly smoked cigars or chewed **Days Work** tobacco. Usually the trips to Orlando were uneventful and we children looked forward to this respite from the isolated existence we had in Dr. Smith's house in the middle of an orange grove.

One Saturday, though, was different. On our way back from Orlando we stopped for something and my daddy turned the ignition off. This wasn't unusual since bathroom runs were common with three young children. We all got back in the car and daddy turned the ignition key. Alas, the engine wouldn't turn over. Daddy knew a little about cars and, fortunately, cars were simple enough then that usually all one needed were a screwdriver and a pair of pliers to fix a problem. He raised the hood and fiddled around a while and tried again. No luck!

"Maybe what we need to do is get the car rolling, pop the clutch and the car might crank," he said.

So, that is what we did.

But someone needed to push and that was a problem. None of us children were large enough or strong enough to do much good. We were on a bit of an incline so daddy got in the driver's side, sat part way in the seat and began pushing with his left leg and foot. Mama often sat in the back seat. Without telling my father, she got out and went around back to help push. After the car rolled about fifteen feet, daddy popped the clutch and the engine roared to life. He hopped the rest of the way into the driver's seat and took off.

That is when we yelled, "Daddy, you're leaving mama. She was pushing and now she is back there in the middle of the road hollering at you to stop so she can get in the car."

Daddy stopped, backed up and mama got into the back seat.

This wasn't the end of the adventure. She berated him the rest of the way home for driving off and leaving her.

"Bully, how come you didn't' see I was not in the car. I will never let you forget leaving me beside the road, Mister."

We kids snickered at each volley but most especially when she said, several times, "You had better not tell any of our friends that you drove off and left me."

Daddy, in his usual calm voice, trying to recover, said, "Luvenia, nobody told you to get out and push and I didn't know you had gotten out of the car."

She didn't let up though and we heard her tell this story many times. I suppose this was one of those so-called teachable moments: *It's best to inform the driver when you get out of the car.* Otherwise, you might be the one who gets left behind, just like mama.

Moving to the City

I'm not sure why my mother and father moved from Vineland, Florida. In January, 1944, when I was one month shy of being seven years old, I found myself part of a sizable caravan moving from the only home I had ever known to Haines City, Florida.

Haines City, with a population of 8,000, counting the chickens, hogs, dogs and cats, was more of a town than a city. My most vivid image of that journey is of the truck, top-heavy with our household items, grazing the lower hanging branches of the citrus trees as we drove down the dirt road, out of the country and into the city.

As we left our rural homestead for the last time, my father said, "I sure hope this ol' truck gets us there without any trouble along the way."

My father, mother, I, Violet and Anjo followed that ol' truck in our family's 1932 tan Chevrolet. Another car belonging to my aunt and uncle followed us and we all made the trip without any problems.

It was in the dead of winter, but the sun shone brightly. These were the days when the temperature in winter rarely went above freezing. We rode the entire distance with the windows wide open.

The trip was only 35 miles so mama did not make her usual delicious snack of Southern fried chicken and homemade biscuits. You can be sure I asked her where my favorite lunch was.

She said, "Boy, we won't be in the car long enough to worry about eating. You'll be there before you know it."

My mother and father rode in the front seat and I was crushed in the middle between my two sisters.

I spent most of my time yelling at them. "Y'all better stop reaching across me trying to hit each other. You can play tit-for-tat after we get to Haines City."

When we got to our wonderful, wooden two-bedroom house, I had no idea that my father had contracted to buy it.

Two months later, after we had settled in and dinner was over, I heard my mother crying. She didn't cry often, and this got my attention because she was sobbing uncontrollably.

"Bully, why on earth did you go and get us in all this debt?"

My soft-spoken father attempted to soothe Mama by saying, "Luvenia, we can do this. We can pay off the house. It may take a while but after we pay for it, we'll own it and it will be ours and not someone else's. In addition, this house plus the three lots cost only $1500.00. Like I always told you, you can never have too much land."

My mother would not be pacified. Finally, my father simply gave up trying to appease her. Many years later when we kids would tease Mama about that night, she would always say that she thought Daddy had said $15,000.

I am not convinced that she misunderstood him.

Even though I still had to sleep in the same room with my sisters, I was happy that I would no longer be in the same bed, sleeping head-to-toe. One who has never had this experience cannot appreciate the great joy of realizing one's siblings had remembered to wash their feet before coming to bed—and the stinky agony if they had not.

That old house saw the birth of my third sister, Lucille and my younger brother, Glenn. Fortunately, Lucille and Glenn came along after my two older sisters had left. Otherwise, we might have had five in one room!

By the time I left home to join the US Air Force in 1959, Haines City had changed a lot. Yet, those years of living in a small town with better schools, caring adult neighbors and many good friends allowed me to "spread my wings" and change my life significantly.

I am sure that move from the country to town gave me the chance to learn and grow in ways that would have been otherwise impossible.

Granddad and the Cane

My grandfather and step-grandmother lived ten streets up from us in Haines City. From the time I was seven until I was fourteen, we had a ritual after church.

Mama would say to us, "You children change out of your Sunday clothes and get ready to go see my daddy."

Grandma was a fair cook except for the awfulness of her Thanksgiving turkey dinners. She had high blood pressure and used very little salt for meals. I guess she never heard of other spices because her bird was always bland and dry.

As I labored at the dinner table, I sometimes said to myself, "This turkey tastes just like the cardboard I once tried to chew."

It was so dry that I had to drink a swallow of water after each bite.

Daddy and mama, always respectful, would eat quietly while engaging in small talk about the weather or fruit crop for the year.

My sister Violet, like the good and quiet young lady she was, soldiered on and even made a complimentary remark at times.

Anjo, on the other hand, in her dry, acerbic and plain-spoken way, said, "Gramma, turkey don't agree with my stomach so if it's alright with you, I'll just eat the vegetables."

If that did not work, Anjo would find a perfect moment to hold her turkey meat under the table for their big ol' German Shepherd. Brutus always eagerly accepted, but I wouldn't be surprised if, on many occasions, he didn't take the turkey outside and bury it alongside his treasured bones

When we weren't eating though, there was never a dull moment because my eighty year old grandpa was a bit of a kidder and prankster. He had lost the two middle fingers on his right hand to an accidental shooting, so he would use his index finger to goose us grandchildren when we walked by. He would also block our paths with his wheelchair as we attempted to run through the house.

His pranks were not always confined to the physical.

My mother used to say, "Boy, you pay attention to your granddaddy and do what he says."

That code language meant we should give him all the respect due one who was older.

Sometimes he would tell interesting stories about growing up in Georgia. Since I was the curious type, I asked questions.

He would laugh and say, "You mean to tell me, you really believed that tall tale I just told?"

I felt stupid for about a minute--little boys can have very short attention spans.

Granddaddy was not always "onstage." I remember sitting on his knee many days while he absent-mindedly rubbed my arm or head with what seemed to be the most loving touch.

I was on alert, though, because I knew this "loving caress" would be followed by nonstop tickling. He would take the index finger on that mangled right hand, ease it under one of my unsuspecting arms and just keep going.

I would laugh until I cried real tears, all the while having fun time with grampaw.

One of his most memorable pranks involved a prop---his walking stick.

Granddaddy would sit quietly and innocently as we grandchildren ran around playing hide and seek and catch-me-if-you-can. Suddenly, and without warning, he would stick out his cane with the crooked end positioned just right to catch us around the ankle. Naturally, we would tumble to the floor and he would laugh heartily.

I would get up and say, "Grandpa, that hurt!"

Violet would quietly cry.

Anjo would get up, walk away and sulk for the next half-hour.

She'd say to mama, "Granddaddy is mean to us."

Sometimes he would hear Anjo. Did that bother him? Absolutely not! He would laugh some more.

Over the years, I got used to his "trip-the-kid-habit."

However, I never could understand why this old man would deliberately set out to hurt us. Later, I figured out that for someone confined to a wheelchair most of the day, it may have been one of the few ways for him to have what he considered fun.

After he passed away, there were so many times I wished he was around, still trying to trip me up. This gruff old man sitting in his wheelchair, having worked all sorts of grueling manual labor in his younger days, had meant so much more to me than someone who made me tumble to the floor.

My Living Room

Today is Sunday, February 13, 1950 and I am sitting in the most significant room in my family's house. We live in a small two-bedroom frame house at 1119 Avenue C, Haines City, Florida, a town that proudly proclaims itself as "The Heart of Florida." Our house isn't much different from all the others in this segregated portion of town where all the African-Americans live.

I can only hope that one day in this country this sort of separation of people based on skin color will stop, but for now this is the custom and practice.

The living room and kitchen floors are covered with multicolored linoleum. The walls are brown plain board, joined together by tongue and groove, and the wood smells rich as if its wet origin, a local swamp, still clings to it.. The darkness of the wood is soothing and peaceful. A few pictures of family members hang on the walls, but most prominent is a picture of Jesus, a staple in most African-American living rooms. This living room is typical of most homes in this little Southern backwater town of 8000 souls, chickens, dogs and cats.

At night, we gather around the RCA radio, which sits against the right wall. We listen to "The Thin Man," "Squeaking Door" and the Friday Night Fights.

"Hey, is Joe Louis still fighting? Maybe we can catch him once more as he beats up on the other big and bad heavyweights," I think.

On the left is a door that is never closed until nightfall – it is my parent's bedroom. And, south of that is the second bedroom where we three children sleep.

The small kitchen adds up to only four rooms for five people.

Dominating the living room is a four legged cast iron heater with a yawning front door and two lids on top. This diabolical invention provides heat for the entire house. There is also a dinner table large enough for all of us to sit around. The dark blue settee I loved so much, one light blue overstuffed Daddy's Chair, a creaky but dependable rocking chair for mama, and two darkly hued straight-backed chairs round out the room.

It is in this room that we congregate for those never-to-be-forgotten Sunday dinners that my mother often seems to fashion out of virtually nothing. It is in this room where the company comes to sit and talk with my parents. We children don't have a lot to say because children are to be seen and not heard, at least not unless someone speaks to us first.

This room is the nerve center of our house. It is here we entertain visitors and do our homework, and many other things.

Our Sunday family dinners took place in this living room. When I close my eyes, I can still see and smell the fried chicken or roast beef, green beans or collard greens, mashed potatoes or rice, all ready to be washed down by the sweetest and tastiest strawberry flavored kool-aid in the world! Right now though, I am thinking, maybe today momma will also top off the Sunday dinner with one of her famous Upside Down Pineapple Cakes.

Last month my friend Sheffield Monroe came over to play on Sunday and my father invited him to stay for dinner.

Sheffield said, "Thanks Mr. Bully, don't mind if I do."

That invitation has already become a part of our family lore. Why would something as innocuous as that qualify as part of a family's story? Well, my father didn't talk in advance with my mother about the quantity of food available and you might have guessed by now that there was just enough food for our small family. When my mother informed my father of this fact, he stood, moved away from the table and surrendered his plate to Sheffield.

Ever since, we have teased my father saying, "Don't mind if I do."

We have made sure he never forgets the words used by Sheffield as he prepared to eat what was supposed to be my father's dinner.

The cast iron heater in this living room also contributes to my life experience in an interesting way.

Some days it is my turn to light the fire in the heater in the mornings. Last week one of those mornings was eventful. I put the wood in atop a bed of newspaper, poured kerosene on the contents and then tossed in a lighted match.

On this cold and dreary morning, the fire didn't start. So, I did something one should never do and which I will never do again. Without giving it too much thought, I removed one of the insert lids, peeped over the opening and looked down into the dark recesses of the heater.

That was the moment the fire chose to leap into existence, burning my face and singing off my eyebrows.

Did my mother pack me up and rush me off to the doctor's office? Not in a million years! Instead, she smeared Blue Seal Vaseline all over my face and sent me to school! I huffed and puffed but off to school I went.

So here it is a week later and I can still hear my schoolmates snicker and tease. One said, "How does it feel to be a walking hamburger?" Another gloated, "If that had been me, my mama would have never made me come to school all burnt up like that."

I had no smart replies to offer. Now, many years later, I wish I had thought of some devastating reply such as, "Well, your mama must not value education like mine. I am sort of glad she insisted that I come to school so I would not miss any of my classes."

When I think about our living room, I am gladdened by thoughts of all the sweet smelling cakes and pies, the pungent and special smell of the Southern Deep Fat Fried Chicken and the good-natured ribbing that occurs around the dinner table. I smile at the memory of Sheffield who has no idea the impact he had on our family. I am saddened when I think that one day my father and mother, with whom I share a special bond, will no longer be with us. This living room will be the province of another family and I can only hope that they have as much fun as we are having.

I will always remember this living room and its warm spirit, a place where I feel at peace with the world. I hope other little boys are as lucky as I am and have the chance to grow up experiencing a special room in which to grow up.

Live on Living Room!

Death of my first and only pet

I was seven when Corpus came into my life and I was ten when he went out of my life. For those three years, he was my constant companion. Corpus was a beautiful golden collie and I loved to pat and rub his fur. He would stand there basking in the glow of my love for him and he'd follow me wherever he could.

He wanted to go to school with me but my mother helped break him of that desire by bribing him with treats just as I'd walk out the door. My school was only two blocks away so I would sometimes run home and play with Corpus during the lunch hour. I had to sneak out because we weren't supposed to leave school during the school day.

Once, he actually went to school with me. But as soon as our principal Mr. Redmond, found out, Corpus was expelled. So, sadly, he was unable to complete even one full day of school!

How could I not want to be with Corpus?

He was male, two feet tall and weighed about 75 pounds. He had a smooth gold and white coat that flowed over him like a beautiful soft river. His tail wagged all the time, especially when I lovingly brushed him once a week.

Corpus loved to play. He would jump on me when he wanted me to toss a ball so he could bring it right back, or when he was ready for one of his spirited runs up and down Avenue C.

His round, clear brown eyes seemed to sense what I wanted to do and most of the time it was what he wanted too---we'd just laze around in the shade of the big mulberry tree in the backyard.

Corpus was no trouble at all. He ate scraps from our meals, even the cauliflower and broccoli I snuck to him under the table. I despised both of those healthy vegetables and he rescued me from having to eat them. He was gentle and barked only when he thought a family member might be in danger or when a stranger approached our house.

One day a tall, ordinary looking white man in a dark blue Chevrolet stopped at our house and offered to buy Corpus.

"I'll give you $50 for him," the man said.

"No sir, I don't want to sell my dog!"

How could a boy and his dog be separated when they were best friends? The man went away but came back a few days later and this time he offered me $75. Again, I said no.

"Mister, I wouldn't sell my dog for any price."

The man had no choice but to give up, and $75 was a lot of money in 1947! He went away but with a scowl on his face.

Two mornings later when I woke up and looked outside for my dog, I saw Corpus lying in the middle of the street in front of our house, not moving. My mother and I rushed to him, but he was dead!

I began to cry and cry and cry. For the next two days, nothing my parents said could stop the tears from flowing out of me like a flash flood.

We had him examined and the veterinarian said that he had enough arsenic in him to kill two full-grown men.

I remember thinking aloud, "Why would anyone kill a dog, especially my Corpus?"

I was mad at the world. Sadness combined with anger put me in a foul mood and made me a difficult person to be around.

I asked my mother, "Why mama? Why would anyone kill my dog?"

Mama said, "Boy, he was a good dog and he was your best friend, but just remember like I told you already, he is bound for Dog Heaven."

We never tried to find out who killed Corpus. And it never occurred to me until much later that perhaps the man who had tried to buy my dog had been the one who poisoned him. As is the case with grief, I slowly accepted that Corpus was gone and I resolved to give him a great send off.

I gave Corpus a funeral a few days later. I told three of my best buddies and they came to help me send Corpus off to Dog Heaven.

On the day of the funeral, we all gathered in the backyard-- Sheffield, Roy Chester, General Parker and me. I borrowed the family

Bible and parroting our minister, Reverend Statom, I began to preach Corpus' funeral. I promised him a wonderful and glorious time in the afterlife and I told him that whoever killed him would surely rot in Hell.

After the service, we carefully laid Corpus in the hole I had dug in the backyard, put some tin over his body and covered him with dirt. We stood around for a while reminiscing about the times we had enjoyed with Corpus.

I grieved for a while longer, but as time passed, I thought about it less and less. I did promise myself, though, that I would never have another pet. The loss of Corpus hurt too much and I didn't want to go through that kind of pain ever again.

It is now many years later and I have been true to my promise.

But, all these years later, I still miss Corpus.

Many times, I use his name when I need a code or password. I guess I still try to keep him close to me in any way I can.

Mr. Jack and his New Chevrolet

When I was growing up, General Motors "ruled the roost" in car sales and popularity. Like most young boys I was, as my mother used to say, "Car crazy." I must admit that I could tell at a glance what the make and model was of virtually any car from quite a distance. When I was nine years old, I witnessed an incident that made an indelible impression on me and made me fully realize what a car could mean to some folks.

While playing in our backyard one afternoon I heard a loud bang. Since such loud noises were unusual in my neighborhood, and since I was a curious kid, I ran to where I thought the sound had originated. It turned out to be at the corner of our street and the main drag a block from our house.

That corner was the intersection of Avenue C and 11th Street. That location had been the scene of several accidents because it was a busy place. Mr. Ernest Carnegie had built a large two-story building at that intersection and in that building was a laundry, pool hall and his plumbing business office. The combination of all that resulted in many cars driving by and often stopping suddenly as they realized they wanted to patronize one of those businesses.

In any case, when I got to that busy corner, I saw two cars entangled in an accident. I realized that the man lying in the street was the notorious Mr. Jack. Mr. Jack was known in our area as the most cantankerous, meanest, one-legged man around. He would "cuss out" anyone at anytime for anything.

The word around town was simply, "don't mess with Mr. Jack." Men who congregated in the small neighborhood area known as "down the street" said they had seen Mr. Jack threaten many younger men and even beat one or two up with nothing but his fists.

Nobody crossed Mr. Jack.

Even so, I was not prepared for what happened shortly after I arrived on the scene.

Several people gathered as people are apt to do when something exciting or disastrous happens. One man hurried over to Mr. Jack.

"Are you okay? Are you hurt?" He asked.

Mr. Jack, a relatively small man, about five feet six inches and 150 pounds, gathered himself up.

"The sonofabitch has wrecked my new Chevrolet."

That's all he said.

We were stunned for a moment and then someone in the rear of the crowd let out a faint chuckle and said in a very low voice, "That's just like Mr. Jack."

The police took reports and got Mr. Jack to the hospital. He wasn't hurt, just tossed out of his new Chevrolet. He actually landed on his wooden leg and that cushioned his fall.

We young boys talked about this for many weeks, first because something exciting and different had happened in our neighborhood. Second, it seemed a shame for a new car to get wrecked, even if it was Mr. Jack's. Third, I was impressed, even at that young age, just how much a man could love his car.

Years later, a fourth reason occurred to me. After all, it was 1946 and rationing was still common since the end of World War II. Cars were still made from materials that were not needed in the war effort, so it was hard to come by a new car, especially for black people who didn't have much money. It's not wise in any circumstances to come between a man and his car, but especially when it's a new Chevrolet.

My First Real Train Ride

When I was nine years old, my Uncle Felix passed away in Summerton, South Carolina. This was in 1946, shortly after World War II had ended, and money and transportation were hard to come by. Since this was my father's only brother, he decided he would do whatever it took to get to the funeral. And, being daddy's boy, I wanted to go. Even though he had little money, he made it possible for me to go with him.

We boarded the train in Haines City.

This was during the golden age of the "iron horse" as it was sometimes called, and the train on the Atlantic Coast Line was impressive, especially to someone young and inexperienced in rail travel. We didn't have enough money to dine in the club car, but even if we had, it was an era of rigid segregation in the Deep South and we wouldn't have been allowed in. So we ate our fried chicken and biscuits that we packed for the over 20-hour trip.

I was surprised and pleased to see black men working the train, mostly as Pullman Porters. They wore fine uniforms and carried themselves with authority and presence. One of them happened to be from my hometown and so I learned what he did when he was away from home "on a run."

The bench seats in this "black people only" coach section were covered with a soft leather-like material and reasonably comfortable. At the back of each seat was a footrest for use by the passenger in the seat behind. Daddy's feet could reach the footrest but my legs were too short.

I will always remember the smell of the coach car. It was a mixture of collected odors from previous runs, current passengers and most noticeable, that of the various bags of food carried by the black passengers inside greasy paper bags.

I could smell fried chicken all the way from Haines City to Summerton, South Carolina.

I had trouble sleeping because I was entranced by the clickety-clack of the train wheels as they passed over the joints in the rails. I finally fell asleep, leaning on daddy's shoulder. The train cars swayed back and forth but with my head always in contact with Daddy, I felt as safe as a baby bird beneath her mother's wings.

After we arrived in Summerton, daddy reconnected with his relatives while my three young male cousins, all about my age, took me with them to visit a neighbor. My problem was that the neighbor lived over a mile away and the mules served as our means of transportation.

I told them I had never ridden a four-legged animal but they assured me I would be fine.

So, they threw a burlap bag over the back of a mule and helped me climb on. Getting me on the mule was not easy. First, they tried to boost me up with their hands. That did not work. John, the eldest cousin, after scratching his head, came up with the solution.

"Let's get some hay bales from the barn, stack them up to make stairs and that ought to work."

Thankfully, that enabled me to mount the mule, a beast that looked to be at least fifteen feet tall.

Was I scared? I wasn't just scared, I was terrified.

However, mustering the bravado young men often display in the presence of peers, I climbed aboard "Old Jim."

The ride there turned out to be uneventful and we played stickball, checkers and hide- and-seek for a few hours.

The ride back home seemed like it was going to be no problem until the mule sighted his home barn. Without any warning, he broke into a gallop. Since I was unschooled in riding, I knew nothing about gripping the mule's sides with my knees. I was bouncing up and down, up and down.

Ultimately, on one of those "ups," I came down and fell off the mule.

I was lying on the ground, my face and mouth full of dust, whimpering like an abused Airedale. My cousins picked me up and started brushing me off.

Levi said, "We had better clean this boy up and stop him from crying before we get back home or we will get a real bad whipping."

That is indeed what they did and they got me to promise that I would not tell anyone about my mishap.

On the way back home, as the train hurtled southward to Haines City, I marveled at the well-dressed passengers as well as the beauty of the green landscape. I sat in my seat; smug with the knowledge that I had a shared story with my cousins that none of the adults would ever know.

I never told my daddy about that fall from the mule, which turned out to be my first and last ride on a four-legged animal.

The School Nurse

When I attended Oakland Elementary and High School, we didn't have our own school nurse, but periodically, about once a month, a travelling nurse would come to our school.

I'm not sure how our prank got started, but like many things when one is young and impetuous, it just seemed to somehow happen. We were outside the Industrial Arts Building, a group of young boys standing around just looking for something mischievous to do. So, when the school nurse drove up and parked on the clay driveway in front of that building, one of us came up with a really devilish idea.

Herbert Davis, one of the oldest, shortest and chubbiest among us said, "Let's put the nurse's car in the sand."

Since we had been going back and forth across the campus getting wood, glue and nails for our class woodworking projects, the six of us apparently had nothing better to do. Although we knew each other from living in the same small neighborhood, the main thing this "gang of six" had in common was Mr. Stevens' Industrial Arts class. Even so, it never occurred to us that any one of us would tattle on the other. Additionally, Herbert was the son of Mr. Cleve Davis, the owner and operator of the neighborhood dry goods store and I figured Herbert had enough "pull" to get us out of trouble if anything went wrong.

To the uninformed, this might not seem like much of a prank. However, the sand in this part of Central Florida was grey, very loose, and very deep.

After the nurse entered the main school building, I and my five "partners in crime" sprang into action. Since we were at most twelve or thirteen years old, we weren't very strong. But there were several of us AND the nurse's car was a precursor of the compact car.

She was driving a Crosley!

We thought, "That thing couldn't be more than eight or ten feet long and maybe three to four feet wide."

It actually was about 48" wide, weighed about 1,000 pounds and had an 80-inch wheelbase.

My little group split into three at the front of the Crosley and three at the rear. We lifted the little car off the clay driveway, carried it over and deposited it into the sandy area next to the driveway. It was so small and light we easily moved the Crosley in less than three minutes. There was some grunting but since we rested a few seconds between "grabs and heaves," we made short work of this deliciously satisfying prank.

Naturally, we ran away to a safe place so we could see what would happen when the nurse returned to her car. It must have been recess because we were able to keep our hiding positions until she came out.

She looked around for her car and seemed puzzled when she saw it. I can imagine her saying to herself, "That is not where I left my car."

She got in, cranked up, put the car in reverse and tried to back out. The wheels spun and dug themselves deeper and deeper into the unforgiving sand. The more she pressed the accelerator pedal, the further down the little Crosley got mired in the sand. She ultimately gave up and reentered the school.

That is when we emerged from our hiding place and stood around nonchalantly.

The nurse came out of the school with the principal, Mr. Henry C. Redmond. He surveyed the situation and knew at once that the car had to be lifted out of the sand.

He looked over to where we were and said, "You boys come on over here and lift this car out of this sand. And, when and if I find out who put this car in the sand, they will certainly get some 'ice cream.'"

"Ice cream" was the 2.5-inch wide horsehide leather barber's strop he kept in his office and with which he dispensed corporal punishment. These were the days when it was common for teachers and principals to administer punishment via straps, belts, and rulers to the open hands of kids who "acted up."

We six hurried over and quickly lifted the car out of the sand and put it back on the clay surface. It was all we could do to avoid giggling while working.

Fortunately, for us, the principal never did find the culprits and even more fortunate and a bit surprising, none of us talked about it except within our little circle. There is no doubt in my mind that if we had bragged about it to other students, word would have gotten back to Mr. Redmond.

Moreover, we would have gotten some "ice cream," the likes of which we would have remembered for a long time.

Smoking in the Outhouse

When I was nine, people around me had started to smoke cigarettes and it always seemed so grown-up. Then some of my friends, who ranged in age from nine to twelve, started sneaking around and smoking. They weren't smoking expensive "store-bought" cigarettes, though. They were rolling their own!

When I was eleven, I decided I was going to smoke me a cigarette, so I did what the others were doing. I got one of the older kids to buy some tobacco in a pouch with a drawstring. I didn't have much money so I didn't get the thin white tissue looking paper needed to roll the tobacco up.

No, I chose to cut a piece out of a brown paper bag about the size of one of those tissues and use that.

I obviously couldn't do it in the open so I went to our outhouse. There I was, sitting on one of the two-holers, carefully and laboriously rolling my very first cigarette.

Little did I know it was nearly my last cigarette!

After I had rolled it and began to close it up, I realized that I wasn't quite clear on exactly how to make the ends of the paper stick together. I supposed that I needed to lick the paper; make it wet and then the ends would stick together.

I did that and held in my hand my first cigarette.

Next I took the book of matches I had "borrowed" from mama's kitchen and grandly struck the match and lit up. My first drag on the cylinder resulted in gagging and coughing like a dog with a fur ball stuck in its throat but I persevered. I was not brave enough to try to inhale the smoke but I was pulling it in and blowing it out.

When I was about one-third through, I heard the back door open. I jumped off the one-hole, looked through a crack and saw my mother heading for the outhouse. I hurriedly threw the cigarette down the hole and quickly opened the door to exit. I met my mom when she was about halfway to the toilet.

I went on into the house as if nothing had happened.

After a while mama came back into the house.

"I thought I smelled smoke in that toilet. Boy, you have not been trying to smoke, have you?"

Thinking very quickly so as to not have to submit to one of mama's famous mulberry switch whippings, I said, "No mama, I was not smoking in there. Anjo was just in there before me so when she comes back home, maybe you should ask her."

I'm not sure if mama ever asked Anjo about "the smoke" but what really mattered is that she didn't ask me again.

And, I never tried to smoke in the outhouse again!

As a matter of fact, I did not smoke again until I was forty-two years old.

I don't think I would have then but by then I was a mid-career Air Force officer and it seemed as if most of the senior officers smoked. Also, the most famous senior officer, General Curtis LeMay, the legendary commander of the Strategic Air Command, smoked large cigars.

So, at forty-two, I started smoking cigars. I know it is trite to say, but I have never inhaled cigar or cigarette smoke. Sometimes I wonder if that gagging and coughing all those years ago somehow rendered me incapable of learning how to inhale and blow those amazing rings of smoke some people can manage.

I know smoking can contribute to the onset of lung cancer and is something no one should do. That is one of the reasons I always discouraged my children from smoking and, although their mother smoked

79

for over fifty years before she quit, neither my son nor daughter has ever smoked.

Gest, the Paper Boy

I don't know if I was all that industrious but I did carry a newspaper for a brief period of time. ***Grit*** was a weekly newspaper that was popular in rural areas throughout the United States during much of the 20th Century.

For more than 125 years, this popular Sunday newspaper offered readers homespun good news, features, fiction, coupons and comics. Nearly one million children sold it, and by 1916 the circulation reached 300,000.

As young entrepreneurs, we children knocked on the doors of small-town homes and were welcomed with a smile and a dime for a weekly edition of ***Grit: America's Greatest Family Newspaper.***

At least some of us were welcomed with a smile and a dime.

I didn't have that experience. I was able to get several families to subscribe and I was very pleased with myself because this meant I would have spending money other than what I earned by collecting empty soda bottles, known in the deep south as bottles of soda water.

At first, the subscribers paid me when I came around to collect. After a short period of time, though, I noted that most of the time when I came to collect, no one was home. It didn't occur to me that people were dodging me, so I soldiered on.

"Mama," I said one day, "our neighbor next door and other families are behind in paying me. I have been going to collect for the paper but they are never at home."

Mama, in her usual understated way, replied, "Maybe they are home but just not answering the door." It had never occurred to me that they could have been at home but simply chose to not answer the door.

As a young, naïve and impressionable boy, I was shocked that older adults who I always thought of as being responsible, might deliberately seek to avoid paying what they owed.

Next time I went around to collect, I paid more attention.

Much to my surprise and chagrin, I saw movement inside some of the homes and, in a few cases, actually saw curtains being drawn. Being persistent, I began to vary my collection times away from my customary Thursday afternoons. I managed to catch a few people that way, but it soon became apparent that I could not continue without going broke!

I was paying for the papers and relying on the subscribers to pay me. When they didn't, I was essentially buying them a Sunday paper!

I told my parents that my great business venture had failed and that I would have to stop carrying the **Grit** newspaper.

They agreed that there was no way to force people to pay me. So my first real part-time job came to an end.

It was the first time I realized that not everyone is dependable or ethical. It didn't stop me from believing in people, but I was more careful in the future about the type of adventure I embarked upon and who I trusted to pay me.

The Sneeze

The food at our Sunday dinners wasn't fancy, but it was both filling and delicious and prepared with all the love my mother could muster. One Sunday she cooked her world famous deep fried chicken, collard greens, cornbread and candied yams. And, we had grape Kool-Aid to drink. We always had something cold to drink with our food. It was only later that I learned many families do not drink anything except water when they eat.

Anyway, the table was loaded down.

My father, Violet and Anjo sat with me as my mother brought food to the table. It wasn't unusual then for moms to spend a lot of dinner getting up and down like yo-yos as they served the family.

Daddy, Robert "Bully" Gest holding Anjo; Violet in the middle; Mama Luvenia Hall Gest, circa 1936

Now, all my life, I have sneezed with tremendous force. My knees would rise fast and hard and the "aaachoo" would gush out with great gusto.

So it was this Sunday that I let loose with a mighty sneeze. My knees rose up from under me with alarming speed and turned the table over onto the floor. Bowls and plates of wonderful hot food crashed into the floor, breaking and spilling onto the linoleum. It looked as if someone had just taken the food and scattered it all over the dining room floor.

Everybody was so stunned, they just sat there. I was mortified.

My father and sisters looked at me as if I had just killed someone – or maybe they were looking **to kill** someone, namely me. My long-suffering mother folded her arms and glared at me. She didn't know what to say and neither did I. I had just ruined dinner for everyone and there was nothing else to eat. No one knew what to say except my sister Anjo, who always had something to say.

She gave me an evil look and said, "Fool, what did you go and do that for?"

Naturally, I had no answer; for how does anyone know why they sneeze. You just do. So, I did what any self-respecting baby of the family would do. I slowly arose from my chair and slunk onto the porch.

I never heard the end of that memorable Sunday. As siblings do, my sisters teased me about dumping the Sunday dinner for many years after. Sometimes now I remember with sadness that both of my sisters passed away before they were 60 years old. Violet, when she was 35 and Anjo, when she was 52.

Violet died in childbirth.

She had given birth to five children in the previous 6 years and she and her husband, JuneBug, had decided to make this sixth child their last. However, she went into a coma after giving birth to the sixth child, a beautiful young girl, and never recovered. I argued for an autopsy but I was outvoted. We believe that complications from high blood pressure and the rapid pregnancies may have been contributing causes of her death.

Anjo had diabetes.

I am almost certain that she did not take the necessary medications to keep her blood sugar under control. Her death was still a surprise. The day before she died, one of her granddaughters, Mercedes, had come to spend a few days with her grand-mom. Anjo lived next door to mama and always came over to the family home no later than nine every morning. This fateful morning she did not come over and mama went next door to check on her. She found three-year old Mercedes wandering around in the house and Anjo dead in her bed.

She had died in her sleep. Her death was attributed to a heart attack.

I really miss my two older sisters, especially that mischievous, stubborn and plain-spoken Anjo. But, then when I remember that Sunday dinner, I smile because even to this day if my family is dining together they are on the alert for one of my never-to-be-forgotten sneezes.

Baptism at Missionary Baptist Church

My mother was a Baptist and my father was a Methodist. When I was young, daddy rarely went to church, but my mother regularly went to Beulah Missionary Baptist Church in Haines City, Florida on Sundays at 11:00 a.m. And when she did, her children went with her!

Because of our church-going history, it was no surprise when my mother asked me one day, "Boy, don't you want to get baptized? After all, you'll soon be twelve and that's when most young folks in this town get baptized.

I said, "Yes, I guess I'm ready."

Frankly, I was more than a little anxious about the whole thing. I had seen other people dunked in the pool underneath the pulpit and since I did not swim, I was more than a little fearful.

Anyway, I decided that since many of my peers had already been baptized and since I hadn't seen anybody drown, I would give it a try.

The next Sunday after another of Reverend Statom's fiery sermons, my mom went to him and told him I was ready to be baptized into the church.

Reverend Statom, a short and light-skinned man, said, "Luvenia, I am so proud of you and all your children and I know Little Robert will make for a good and faithful church member."

I had seen baptisms so I knew what to expect but that doesn't mean that I was not unsure about the whole thing. One of my closest friends had recently drowned in the neighborhood lake and I was deathly afraid of doing the same thing. I suppose I knew the people in the church would not let me sink and die, but fear can be paralyzing.

After months of imagining myself under water, the Sunday of my baptism arrived. I wore everyday clothes that were covered by a long, flowing white cotton robe.

I and four other youngsters were led to the altar. I knew my mother, two sisters and the whole church congregation was looking to see how we would do.

I, on the other hand, was thinking, "This must be just like our rooster felt when he saw my daddy coming toward him with the hatchet."

The baptismal font was a pool underneath the stage on which the pulpit sat. The deacons removed the covering floor of the font and there it was -- the water.

My guess is that I was a lot more concerned than the other children.

My mother had forbidden me to get myself in more water than could fit into a Number 3 tin tub, where I bathed cramped up every night. I was little but still a tub that size was just too small. I couldn't swim and I was terrified of getting into water over my head.

Ever since my friend had drowned the previous summer, Mama had decided that since I too couldn't swim, she would protect me by making sure I didn't get into any water unless it was to get me clean.

I stood looking at this pool of water, maybe four or five feet deep, and to me it might as well have been the Atlantic Ocean.

Then, it was my turn.

Reverend Statom took me by the hand and led me down the steps. He made sure my footing was firm, asked me if I was ready to be baptized, said a prayer, pinched my nose together and dunked me under the water.

It seemed an eternity.

I came up sputtering and spitting. My relatives led me away, dried me off and delivered me to my mother who was smiling broadly and happily.

My Aunt Evelyn who played the piano better than even Fats Waller, laid her hands on me and said, "Thank you Jesus, thank you Jesus for saving this boy."

I mustered a weak smile, thanking Jesus for saving me, too. He didn't let me sink. I was just glad to come out alive. I didn't feel any different. I didn't detect heated Christian blood flowing through my veins.

However, at least I had as the pastor always said at these baptisms, "Joined the Christian band."

Singing in the Choir

After I was baptized at age twelve, Reverend Statom asked me to join the youth choir. Before this, I had not known I was tone deaf and, as some said, "Could not carry a tune in a water bucket."

So, I willingly joined the choir because many of my friends were already members.

I went to my first choir practice with great anticipation because I had always admired the beautiful harmony and wonderful sounds that emanated from the men's choir. My voice had not changed yet as boy's voices do with puberty, so as I began to sing along with the others, I realized how awful I sounded!

My voice was high and ragged and I croaked like the fat sea green frog I had seen a few days earlier. My first practice was a total disaster.

I returned home and asked my mother if I could quit the church choir.

"Why?" she asked. Because, I said, "I sound terrible."

With all the wisdom of a loving mother, mama replied, "It's normal for your voice to sound like it does before it changes to a man's."

I wasn't convinced or soothed, but I did return to the next practice and, in the interim, performed with the youth choir that next Sunday morning. As before, I was horrified by the sounds that came out when I attempted to sing. The screeching sounds made me think of a terrible automobile accident; tires squealing, metal crashing against metal; everything about a car wreck but the smell of gasoline spilling onto the road surface.

Therefore, I did what I thought I had to do. I approached my Aunt Evelyn, the choir director and pianist, and explained my situation.

"Please talk to mom and convince her that I should wait a few years until my voice changes and I don't sound like a shrieking owl." She agreed and, fortunately, so did my mother.

My voice did indeed change when I was almost fourteen but that did not help my singing. I was still tone deaf and churchgoers in the pews still shuffled about uncomfortably when I attempted to sing.

This marked the end of my singing career and never again did I try to sing in a group. I don't even let loose in the shower! I learned a valuable lesson from this---not all people can do all things. If you don't have the vocal cords, admit that sometimes, "Failure is an option."

Work After School

When I was 12, I thought of myself as the "Little Gest Boy." After school, I would go to the orange groves of Central Florida to help my daddy. This particular day I am riding my bike to where the men are pickin' fruit.

I find my dad and, even though I'm all of 5' 2" and weigh at most 120 pounds, I strap the heavy extra bag he has brought to work diagonally across my shoulder. When it's full and weighing 90 pounds, the bottom of it drags the ground as I move from one spot to another.

My Dad says, "Okay boy, get that bag busy working the ground while I get the ladder."

I begin picking the fallen Valencia Oranges I can reach. This is called "grounding." My daddy uses a ladder that sometimes reaches 25 feet into the sky. To me, it seems as if the ladder goes all the way to heaven, where it is just as blue and clear as this Florida day.

My father is only six inches taller than me, but he is fully grown and has done manual labor all his life. His same-size bag sways more than a foot from the ground and he carries it with ease and grace. He moves around the trees, picking all he can from either side before he moves the ladder to another setting and then another setting until the tree is picked clean. The ladder occasionally sways and twists if not leaned properly against the tree, but my daddy sets it right. Even if the ladder is a little off center, he "rides" it until it's in place.

Picking oranges is backbreaking work. My father and I quickly snap the orbs from the stubborn tree stems and drop them into the canvas bag with the flap at the bottom. We do this until our bags are full. Then we carry, or in my case drag, the bags to a two-compartment box, flip open the flap and dump the ranges until the box is full. My bag leaves a two-foot wide trail through the grey, hot sand. My father and I do this over and over for the sum of fifteen cents a box.

I am too small and weak to do a lot, but I help as much as I can because our family needs all the money we can get. My Daddy picks fruit five days a week and my mother stays home and takes care of the house and us children. We work hard, me getting the tree "grounded" while Daddy "tops" it. We often pick 20 or 30 boxes before it is time to head home.

Little did the "Little Gest boy" know at the time that these were the "good old days!"

After graduating from high school at fifteen, I had no money for college, so I returned to the citrus groves as a laborer to earn what I needed to continue my education. I became skilled enough at 'pickin' fruit until I could manage 140 boxes per day. By now, the pay was up to a "whopping" seventeen cents a box, so on good days I could earn as much as twenty-three dollars. That might not seem like much but if one made eighty dollars a workweek, he was considered a great fruit picker.

Some days, after I had picked over a hundred boxes, I would cramp up due to dehydration and have to quit before the workday was over. When I got home, my mother would say, "Come here boy and lay on the sofa so I can work on you." Lovingly, she would massage my legs and arms with kerosene until the large cramped up muscles relaxed. Then I would take a hot bath in the Number Three Tin Tub if I hadn't fallen asleep right after dinner.

The next day, I would get up at first light, catch the labor bus, go with the older men to the groves and do it all over again-- all the while thinking about getting to college so I would never in my lifetime have to work at 'pickin' fruit for a living.

I know how often my daddy would say, "Hard work is honorable and never killed anybody." I knew he was right, but I figured there were plenty of ways to work hard and I intended to see what they were!

The Tennis Shoes

The first day of P.E. class the instructor looked at the pimply-faced adolescents before him and much like a drill sergeant said, "I am going to whip you boys into shape. Y'all are gonna' need some tennis shoes. Converse shoes will be okay but any brand will do as long as they can stand up to the rigors I intend to put you through."

There I stood, all of 12 years old, poor as a church mouse, with no tennis shoes in my wardrobe and wondering what to do. My family was unable to buy tennis shoes for me, but I had to have them in order to participate in this mandatory class. Since my grades in all other subjects were very good, I was very afraid P.E. would bring me down.

Later that day, my classmate Cleve Davis, whose father owned and operated the local dry goods store in the black community, privately offered me a pair of sneakers that he no longer used.

I was ecstatic!

I took the shoes and thanked him profusely.

I treasured those shoes because now I could participate in gym with all the other boys.

Unfortunately, I had used them for only a week when Cleve "outed" me in front of all the other boys in our gym class.

He said, "Robert, how are those tennis shoes I gave you doing for you?"

I was mortified. You can imagine the shame I felt.

All eyes were on Cleve and me. They looked back and forth, from me to him and then back again.

I fell into a blue funk and thought about it for a day. I really needed those shoes, but I knew my pride came first.

So in Gym class the next day, with the entire class looking on, I drew myself up to my full five feet, walked over to Cleve and said, "Here, I no longer want your shoes."

Cleve was stunned. He tried to get me to keep them, "No Robert, I gave them to you and I want you to have them."

I was not to be denied. I insisted that he take them and so he did. It was more important to me that I maintain my dignity than own gym shoes.

When I told my mother what I had done, she said, "Good for you! We may be poor but we have our pride. And further, one of these days you'll be able to buy and sell Cleve Davis."

I learned two lessons from this humiliation.

First, one should always do what is necessary to maintain his self-esteem. Without self-esteem one can find his self-worth diminished, confidence weakened and likelihood of future success decreased.

Second, when someone gives a gift, the good deed loses its intrinsic value when one boasts about doing it. Doing a good deed should be about humility and not bragging about what one has done.

Why I Dislike Raw Onions

Each June, when the citrus fruit was all harvested in Florida and there was no more manual labor available, we went "on the season." It was likely called "on the season" because we were following the seasons in order to get work so we could survive. We would join several other families and single folks and drive often unreliable cars from Florida to New York.

Sometimes we worked our way up the East Coast, beginning in Maryland where we picked tomatoes, beans, cucumbers, potatoes or anything else that grew out of the ground that afforded farm work for unskilled laborers. Most often, though, we went directly to New York, sometimes Long Island where we stayed the entire summer.

On Long Island (Shelter Island, Greenport, Mattituck, Laurel, et. al.) we worked in white potatoes, strawberries, tomatoes and hay. In Upstate New York, if we went all the way to the Sodus area, we mostly picked cherries and apples. But in Middletown, which is closer to New York City, we often worked in onions.

I must have been thirteen years old the first year we went to Middletown.

I worked alongside my daddy from sun up to sun down, five days a week and half a day on Saturday. The onions grew in black loamy soil that was very loose. After the onions were ready for harvest, the farm owner sprayed the tops of the onions so the leafy part turned brown, died and fell over. The bulb of course was unharmed and below ground.

We laborers would then come along with very sharp shears, pull the onion bulb plant up by the leafy part, hold the whole thing over a box and cut the bulb loose from the rest of the plant. Like most common labor work, we were paid by the number of boxes we managed to fill. It was called "piece work."

The work was hard, dirty and exhausting.

We were on our knees, hopefully wearing knee pads, crawling down the rows of onions and quite often cutting our hands through the gloves some of us were lucky enough to wear. This was bad enough! But, in addition, the onion juice and the odor that originated from the onion field would work its way into the pores of my skin.

After the workday was over I'd take a long hot bath. And, on the weekend, I would often take two baths on both Saturday and Sunday. Unfortunately, I would still smell like onions. I couldn't get away from it.

I grew to hate onion odor.

Before this adventure, I would often eat raw onion slices on burgers my mother made. But because of my time in the onion fields of Upstate New York, I made myself a solemn promise that if I ever got away from onion fields, I would never again eat onions. In later years, I did get around to eating them cooked or sautéed , but never again have I eaten raw onions.

Making Mulberry Wine

In Haines City, Florida, lemon and lime trees gathered around the front of our house and orange, grapefruit, tangerine and mulberry lined our backyard. In the summer when it was hot, the cacophony of citrus smells seemed to overpower one's other five senses. The fruit trees were burdened with their bounty from October of one year to June of the following year; trees standing tall and strong but ready to yield their gifts. Even so, we rarely ate the fruit in front of us, for the lemon and lime was too bitter and we had our fill of citrus since we made our living "pickin' fruit" in the groves.

I loved the large mulberry tree that sat squarely and majestically in the middle of the backyard, halfway between our house and the one-room utility building in back of our lot. Some days I would eat mulberries until my lips and fingers turned purple and my stomach expanded like a balloon. Sometimes I thought I would burst wide open.

My mother would periodically preserve mulberries and make mulberry jam/jelly in Mason Jars. Store-bought jams and jellies just don't measure up to my mother's---she far outclassed all of them.

When I was 12, I had heard how my father made wine from various fruits, so I asked him if I could make a little mulberry wine.

He said, "Okay, but you talk to me before you try to drink any."

He then explained the process to me. He said, "first you get some sugar, yeast, a gallon jug and of course some mulberries. Then you put the berries in first, and then in order, fill the jug about halfway with water and finally put in the sugar and yeast. Now, all you need to do is set the jug somewhere and wait."

Armed with the necessary information, I "borrowed" some sugar and yeast from my mother and got myself a gallon jug. I picked about a quart of mulberries and put them in the jug along with the sugar and yeast and some water. I knew I would have to set it aside and wait for it to ferment. I figured the logical place to store it was that utility building, so with a flourish, I deposited my mini-wine still there.

Unfortunately, I don't know if I forgot about it or I didn't ask my daddy how long I should leave this concoction. In any case, about two weeks later I was fooling around in the backyard when I heard a loud explosion that seemed to come from the utility building. I ran to our quaint little unassuming plank utility building, opened the door and was greeted with a terrible surprise. All I could see was a roomful of purple liquid and mush dripping from the ceiling and running down the walls forming its own river of beautiful mulberry remains. Shards of glass were scattered around the room like pieces of sparkly diamond. My mulberry wine had reached its full potential. The contents of the jug had fermented until the gallon jug could not contain its swollen mash. Sadly, the wine "makins" that had had so much potential had insisted on more room to grow and would now never be enjoyed by me or anyone else.

I stood there in that little building for at least five minutes wondering what to do next. Finally, I concluded that my only choice was to tell my mother what had happened. Since she had not been keen on my making wine in the first place, I got no sympathy from her.

Instead, she gave me a stern look and said, "Well, go back and clean it all up."

It took me an hour of working gingerly to clean up "my mess."

I never again made mulberry wine. I stuck to just eating the mulberries.

Cleaned the Family Car too good

Mr. Charlie, who was Miz Ida's husband, prided himself on having one of the cleanest and shiniest cars in the neighborhood. After all, if he was to maintain his standing as one of the premier number runners, he needed to drive a clean and shiny car.

And I was the one who cleaned and shined it!

When it became apparent that I was getting pretty good at washing cars, my father had this great idea ---great for him but not so great for me. He suggested it was time for me to wash the family car. Like most children, I was eager and willing to work away from home, but if a parent asked, it seemed like unfair labor.

Even though I knew that if I did a good job, I would become the permanent car washer in the family, I still set out to do my best.

Little did I know how good my best would be.

I washed the car with great care. I swept out the interior and washed the windows with Windex and newspaper pages. When I finished, I stepped back and admired my work.

Daddy came out and asked if I wanted to go to town with him. There was nothing I wanted to do more than ride in the car with my daddy.

We drove up Avenue C and turned left on Eleventh Street. We crossed the railroad tracks and got on the road leading past the concrete plant and Cook Fruit Company. As we were passing Cook's, my daddy turned to spit out the window--he often chewed tobacco when he wasn't smoking a cigar or pipe. But I had left the windows up and the tobacco mess splattered up against the window and started a slow journey down into the door frame.

Fortunately, my father was even-tempered and not easily rattled. Actually, I don't think I ever heard him utter a word of profanity or raise his voice in anger. But this time what he said was absolutely amazing.

He turned to me as I sat petrified next to him and said, "Boy, you did too good a job washing this car, especially the windows."

A Penny Saved; a Penny Lost

When I was a young boy, my father earned the family income and my stay-at-home mother managed the money. Both of them had lived through the Great Depression so money management was a big thing with them. Sometimes, though, it seemed that my mother had a tendency to take things to the extreme-- at least according to my father.

One example involved buying groceries. Most of the time we used the Publix Supermarket in town, but meats were expensive there. So when my mother learned that there was a meat market selling cheaper beef, she decided to make that her destination. Consequently, about once or twice a month, daddy would drive mama 48 miles roundtrip to Bartow where she would carefully purchase the meat she needed.

At first, daddy did this without complaint. But one day, just before it was time to leave, I heard daddy say, "Luvenia, why don't we just buy the meat downtown?"

"Bully, you know that meat downtown costs a lot more and we have three kids in this house who eat a lot of meat."

Daddy, who had given this considerable thought, said, "Well, the meat might be a little cheaper, but by the time we include the cost of the gas and oil, the wear and tear on the car, plus the time it takes to drive there and back, I don't think we are saving all that much."

Without the facts on her side, and without missing a beat, she said, "I don't care; the meat over there is better and it is cheaper so we are going."

Daddy was always a quiet, non-argumentative type so he gave in and drove her over to Bartow. At twelve, I was old enough to ask reasonable questions, so I asked daddy why he gave in when he was right. His answer has stood me in good stead over the years.

"Boy, your mama is not prepared to listen to facts and if I insist, it will only lead to an argument. And, in the long run, it's just not worth it. Sometimes you give in even when you know you're right. Sometimes it is best to keep the peace especially when the battle is not worth the cost."

Daddy drove mama to Bartow for several more years.

I can truthfully say there have been times when I knew I was right but others have insisted they were right. When the issue was significant and worth the cost, I pushed ahead and argued my point. When it didn't hurt me, I learned to simply "go along to get along."

On those occasions, I may have "lost a penny," but looking back, I actually "saved a penny."

Saving a penny means I learned that people have feelings and egos that sometimes need to be considered. I realized that if the matter was not earth-shattering or game-changing, it was often wiser to not belabor the issue, and leave the other person intact by allowing them to "save face."

After all, to paraphrase Sun Tzu in his treatise on the 'Art of War' written in 6th Century B.C., "What value is it in winning the battle only to lose the war?"

The Christmas Tree

The custom at my school for Christmas was to procure a tree from the wooded areas relatively nearby. Imagine my great joy to discover that Principal Henry C. Redmond asked me to be a member of the group of five boys chosen for the task.

It was 1950 and I was thirteen years old. We chosen boys were known to be responsible, good students. I was actually referred to as that "good little Gest boy."

We left school shortly after the day began with our two axes. We walked about three miles to a wooded area and looked around a bit. Out of the blue, Joe Wiley said, "Let's go for a quick swim in Tower Lake."

So, we did.

Although we were familiar with each other's anatomy from showering together after Gym Class, we did keep our shorts on. There we were, five young boys frolicking in the lake, having the time of our lives. Since I could not swim, I waded near the edge while the other four swam at least fifty feet out.

Finally, after an hour in the lake, we emerged, dried off, put our clothes back on and set out to find the school Christmas tree.

Before we could begin our task, we saw a mule wandering about. Not surprisingly, we once again were distracted.

Richard Johnson said, "How about we catch that mule and take turns riding him."

So, we did, for an hour and a half!

Then we ate the lunches we had brought.

About 2 pm, we began to search in earnest for a tree that would grace our auditorium for the next several weeks. As luck would have it, we settled on what was perhaps the scrawniest and scraggliest tree in the area.

We began to cut it down.

Since we were incorrigible by now, I suggested we use the mule to drag the tree at least part of the way back to school. We were so involved in our "fun", we failed to see that someone had observed our antics.

We used the mule to drag the tree out of the wooded area to the nearest clay road and then we took turns dragging the tree back to the campus.

Unfortunately, by the time we got back, the school day had ended.

Mr. Redmond was waiting for us.

"Boys," he said, "I know what you've been doing all day and you have shamed me and the entire school. Mr. Kingston, who owns the mule you all rode, called and told me he saw you all riding his mule."

After a vigorous tongue-lashing, Mr. Redmond lined all of us up along a wall of his office for what he famously called a treat of some of his "ice cream," which was his two and a half inch leather horsehide barber's strop. We cringed because he was known to wield that strop in a wicked fashion.

He proceeded to "walk the line," meting out some of the worst corporal punishment of my young life. By the time he had finished scolding us and giving out the "ice cream," he told us to go home and never try anything like this again.

Little did I know that my day wasn't over. When I arrived home, my mother already knew about my daylong misadventure. Predictably, she ordered me into the backyard to our imposing mulberry tree to cut her a switch.

"Boy, you had better get me a good one," she said.

I knew better than to come back with a puny switch so I cut a prodigious one, which she promptly trimmed so that only the flexible and unforgiving branch was left.

Mama then swung it through the air a few times to test it. This fearsome switch whistled as it cut through the humid Florida air like a knife cutting through warm butter.

She had me stand in front of her and began to lash me at least ten times across my backside, talking to me all the while. When she finally stopped, I had a red, welted, stinging bottom to accompany the swollen, red hands provided by Mr. Redmond.

I never forgot the <u>Christmas Tree</u> adventure and naturally **never** volunteered to go procure another tree for the school. The shame of what I had done plus the unmerciful teasing by my schoolmates made an indelible mark on me and taught me that it was less painful to be that "good little Gest boy."

On Becoming a Man

It's evident in my other tales that my sister Violet was quiet and easygoing and never gave my parents or me any trouble. Anjo, on the other hand, was a rebel, a constant problem for my parents and a nemesis to me. Today, I would probably call her a "frenemy"-- part friend and part enemy. Since I was four years younger and she was stronger than me, Anjo often roughed me up.

Anjo would regularly take my head between her hands and bang it up against the wall. And she wasn't stupid—she did it when my mother or father weren't around. She would get angry with me for no reason and punch me in the stomach or on the back of the head or even worse. This went on from the time I was eight until I was thirteen.

And then, one day it stopped!

For some reason on that particular day when she began her usual "it's fun to bang my head against a wall" routine, I didn't take it without a whimper while begging her to stop. On this momentous day, I grabbed her around the waist and started to squeeze. I mounted what would be considered a "bear hug." I "hugged" her around the waist as hard as my puny arms could manage. Much to my surprise, after only a few moments, she began to gasp.

"Turn me loose fool."

In answer, I ratcheted up the pressure, squeezing as hard as I could. My adrenaline likely gave me more strength than I normally could have mustered.

Wheezing loudly now, she managed to whisper between my squeezes, "Let me go, let me go boy." I tightened my grip, reveling in my newfound strength and said to her, "I knew this day would come and I intend to make you pay."

I sensed that there was less pressure on the sides of my long-suffering head!

After what seemed like forever, her grip on my head loosened and I knew then I was onto something.

I squeezed even harder.

That is when she screamed for my father, who was at the back of the house.

"Daddy, come get this crazy boy off me."

I squeezed some more. Daddy came to see what the fuss was all about.

"Turn her loose boy; what do you think you're doing?" Daddy moved closer, "Let that gal go."

"Anjo has been abusing and misusing me forever and now that I'm strong enough to fight her back, I'm doing it!"

Daddy was unmoved.

"Let her go I said."

Reluctantly, I loosened my grip and gradually let her go.

"You better promise that you'll never hurt me again," I said.

Between gasps, she said, "Yeah, okay, I didn't' hurt you that much. What a sissy fool."

I let her go and stepped back.

When she was finally free, and determined to have the last word, she whispered so Daddy couldn't hear, "In addition to being a sissy, you're a wimpy punk too."

There are no words to express the sense of satisfaction and pleasure I felt at that moment. I was ecstatic!

I didn't think of it then as passing into puberty on my road to manhood, or as a teen "feeling his oats." I was just happy that my days of being roughed up by Anjo were over and maybe, just maybe, my puny arms could protect me in the future.

The Street in Front of Our House

Our unpretentious house at 1119 Avenue C sat on an unremarkable street in a forgotten part of town. Although our small town had 8,000 inhabitants, the African-American people lived in just two segregated sections of the town--Oakland and The Hill. W lived in Oakland right next to the railroad tracks.

Youngsters like to play and have fun, and when they are young they don't think about or see things the way adults might. It never occurred to me that the reason for the poor conditions of our streets and lights might be due to our ethnicity. We had no sewer system, so we were forced to dig and construct septic tanks. Most of the streets in Oakland were made of red clay, and the street in front of our house was no exception. Periodically, the city grading machine would come out and grade the red clay in front of our house, but often the holes went unfilled. When it rained, as it often does in Central Florida, the red clay turned to red mud and the holes turned into pools of dirty water.

Now, looking back, I understand why the street in front of our house was unpaved with huge holes. After all, we were black and we had no political or economic clout. We were living in a shameful portion of America's history, when the lynching of black folk was commonplace in the Deep South. I would hear my parents talk in low tones about the Night Riders who sometimes swept through black neighborhoods and terrorized the people. Because I was so young, I didn't understand, but in later years it all became clear.

And yet that red clay mud was one of my favorite amusements. I would go outside and jump into one of those muddy rain filled holes. I'd turn partially red from the mud, and the warm rain water would seep between my toes like gooey cookie dough.

It felt fantastic.

Sometimes the kids next door and across the street would join in.

Naturally, my mother wasn't happy having to supervise my nighttime bath to make sure I had gotten the mud out of my pores. It was also her task to wash the clothes I'd been wearing while sloshing around in the mud and water. Washing me and the clothes left my mother with a Number 3 Tin Tub stained in red and full of grainy water and silt. She tried to punish me, but since most of us played in the red clay mud, she ultimately just let me know from time-to-time how displeased she was.

How true it is that despite the gravity of situations, children seem to find the fun in it. Perhaps that is their gift, and quite often, it is their gift to us. It may behoove us to remember that the next time we see a child laughing in a situation that seems bleak. Remembering those times helps me to see as I did when I was a child. It's something we should all do no matter how old we get!

After all, red clay mud can be warm and inviting and pothole puddles can bring comfort and joy.

Saturday Afternoon at the Movies

I lived in a fairly small, segregated neighborhood in Haines City, Florida called Oakland. It was one of the two areas where back folks were concentrated. The other was called The Hill. During the years from 1944 – 1954, all services were available in one of these two communities. So we had grocery stores, barbershops, dry cleaners, dry goods stores, pool rooms, gas stations, and a drugstore that did not fill prescriptions. Fortunately, especially for us kids, we also had a theater that showed movies on Friday night and Saturday afternoons and nights. Going to a "show" was one of the highlights of our week.

Even though money was always in short supply, sometimes I could get my parents to give me twenty five cents that wasn't needed for something more important and I would go to a show. I'd step up to the ticket window and for the princely sum of ten cents, I'd get in. Then I would use the remaining fifteen cents to buy popcorn and a soda water. We didn't call it "pop" then.

Sometimes, I would go next door to Mr. Ben's drugstore and buy a gingerbread cookie instead of popcorn. That cookie cost no more than five cents and it must have been at least five inches in diameter. I would take my seat in the theater along with the others who were lucky enough to come into possession of the admission price and we would excitedly wait to see what wonders the big screen brought us that week.

We especially eagerly anticipated the serials. First we saw previews of coming attractions followed by a newsreel, and then came a cartoon like Bugs Bunny. The serial came next and then the main attraction. The newsreel news, though somewhat dated, gave us an idea of what was happening in the world. The serials were much like soap operas since its stories evolved with each cliffhanging segment ending abruptly and not being picked up until the following week. We couldn't wait to find out what Little Beaver, a sidekick of the famous cowboy Red Ryder, would do this week. Those were also the days of Zorro, Hopalong Cassidy and Gene Autry, the singing cowboy!

We would sit transfixed by the images, often yelling at the good guy, "Look out fool, there is someone behind you." Of course we knew the star couldn't hear us, but we participated anyway.

We sometimes stuck chewing gum under the seats and spilled our soda on the floor, making it sticky. I am sure the theatre proprietor had a few choice words to say while cleaning up after each movie. By that time we were long gone, talking up a storm about what we had just seen. And, we would talk about it all week while wondering if we would be able to get the price of admission for the coming weekend.

In later years, after integration, the once prosperous black businessmen disappeared from these two communities. No longer were they able to operate profitably because of the competition from the stores downtown and at the mall. These wonderful establishments closed and were boarded-up, now victims of racial progress!

Even now, when I go home it feels as if something is missing and I find myself longing for what we fondly refer to as "the good old days." I wonder if children growing up today ever experience the carefree enjoyment of living in a completely supportive environment.

The utter joy and complete freedom to get together with other young children and go to the neighborhood picture show, with no adult supervision, was liberating. We took it for granted. Unfortunately, children today aren't able to enjoy the kind of experience we had at the Saturday afternoon movies.

Miz Ida Across the Street

Across the street from us lived the Carrs. The man occasionally worked in the groves picking citrus fruit but he also "ran the numbers." In other words, he sold lottery tickets in an illegal and under-the-cover numbers operation. I think the kingpins of this widespread criminal enterprise were Cuban for this "game" was called "Bolita."

His wife, Ida was a bit older than my mother and she was a stay-at-home wife. We all called her "Miz Ida." In the neighborhood, she was known to involve herself in the lives of others. She and Mr. Charlie had no children of their own and that may have been part of the reason she considered us part of her extended family.

Miz Ida was a small woman; five feet two inches at most. Unlike my mother who had long thick black hair, Miz Ida had short graying hair that she usually wore tied in a bun at the back. This gave her the "librarian" or "school teacher" look which to most of us children, was fearsome.

And, when she talked, she often stopped to purse her lips. Sometimes it even sounded as if she was smacking her lips. Miz Ida was a force to be reckoned with.

I remember with great joy when she would come to our house and interfere to my advantage.

My mother, though, wasn't always happy to see Miz Ida. Miz Ida coming through the door any time of day and either starting her own conversation or joining in one that we were into before she arrived. I'm sure she meant well, but that didn't help my mother feel better about her interfering.

There were days when she would come over and see my mother doing something and quickly share with my mother everything she was doing wrong.

"Luvenia, that's not the best way to do those flowers. What you ought to do is cut them back almost to the root and that way when they grow out, they will be fuller."

My mother would bite her tongue to keep from saying more. "Okay Miz Ida that may be what I should do."

You see, even though my mom was only five or ten years younger, in those days you referred to anyone older than you as either Mister or Mrs. And, my mother was no exception.

She would take to muttering under her breath, though, and after Miz Ida had left, mama would say out loud, "That old woman ought to mind her own business and stop coming over here telling me what to do."

There were days, though, when I was glad to see Miz Ida. She would often come over around breakfast time.

And, she would often remonstrate with my mother, "Luvenia, you know that boy is a growing. Why in the world are you scrambling only three eggs for him? Give that boy six eggs and if you don't have enough eggs, I'll go home and get you some."

Knowing how much my mother disliked Miz Ida's nosiness and often-unwanted involvement in her life, I took great pains to hide my gleeful smile. After all, I was about to get a more filling breakfast!

Miz Ida lived a long and "interfering" life and I was sad when she died. There was no longer "the lady across the street" who took a personal interest in the care and feeding of a neighbor's child. The neighbors seemed less personal and less involved and I so missed that extra ounce of caring.

Many times since then when I heard the expression, "It takes a village to raise a child", I always thought of Miz Ida. She was meddlesome and often aggravated my mother, but I am sure she meant well and did what she thought was best for the neighborhood children.

Your Granddaddy Has Been Shot

We were making small talk on our front porch one spring day in 1951 when a friend rushed up to the house and said to us, "Luvenia, your daddy's been shot and is bleeding all over the place."

Without a moment's hesitation, my mother jumped up, snatched open the flimsy screen door and ran down the steps.

Under the circumstances, it might not seem unusual for someone to run eight blocks when her father has been shot, but mama, at five feet and 250 pounds, <u>never</u> ran. I was so stunned, I took off after her. Even though I was a mere lad of 14 and fit, I had a difficult time matching mama's pace all the way to my grandfather's house.

When we arrived, breathless, mama asked her stepmother Lula Hall, "How is he? Is he all right? Is he dead?

"Calm down. He got the middle three fingers on his right hand blown off. The shooter thought your daddy was someone else and he's already been arrested."

We never spoke much of that day as the day granddaddy got shot. Until mama died in 1993, it was known as the day mama ran eight blocks nonstop.

She would smile and say, "Between my adrenaline pumping and God pushing from behind, there was no way I wasn't going to be able to run. My weight, my arthritis—nothing was going to stop me!"

Do Not Back Out Into a Main Street

Like most youngsters beyond sandlot baseball age, I looked forward to getting my driver's license. This was about the time that I also started to see girls in a different light. I could just visualize myself borrowing the family car and taking my girlfriend to the drive-in movie five miles outside town.

In 1952, I was fifteen years old, and in Florida I could get a Junior Operator License. My father had been the one training me and I was confident I could pass the test. After all, I studied the driver manual for weeks before turning fifteen.

At last, the big day came.

Daddy took me down to the testing station and turned me loose on the officials. I was as nervous as a long-tailed cat in a roomful of rocking chairs. Despite my jitters, I was determined to pass so I could at last enjoy the status symbol and "pass to freedom" of a driver's license.

Each phase of the driving test was uneventful until I came to the final part where I was required to parallel park. I had practiced it many times, so even though I was reluctant, I was sure I could do it. Tentatively and with great anticipation, I pulled ahead of the cones, put the gear into reverse and amazingly backed in between the cones on the very first try.

The testing official said, "I am surprised that you did so well because it was obvious that you were a bit nervous."

I stammered and said, "Thank you sir."

So a mere two days after turning fifteen, I could legally drive and I couldn't wait to get on the road.

Fortunately, the next day my father decided to go fishing and he asked me if I wanted to drive us to the lake! Of course, I said YES almost before he got the question out of his mouth. I think now that my father, who almost never went fishing, might have decided to that day so I could try out my new "driving wings." I was behind the wheel and ready to go even though not all my driving would be done on backcountry clay roads.

As we left our house, Daddy said we needed to stop and get gas. Mr. Ben, who ran the neighborhood drug store, had a gas pump that daddy used quite often so that is where I headed. Mr. Ben's gas pump was on the right side of a side street and fairly close to a main street -- 11th Street -- which ran through our entire Oakland neighborhood. I drove up to the pump and daddy got out and pumped the gas. When he got back in, I started to drive down the side street intending to go around the block, get back on 11th Street and continue on to the lake.

However, daddy scowled at me and said, "Back up boy, don't go all that distance around the block."

I had read the driver manual carefully before getting my license, so I told him, "Daddy, I am not supposed to back out into a main street."

He said, "Aw pshaw, go ahead and back out."

So, I did.

Imagine my surprise and chagrin when as soon as I had backed halfway into 11th Street, a police car pulled up beside me and waved for me to stop. Naturally, I did. The policeman asked for my driver's license. Even though I was so proud of my license that I had placed it in a prominent part of my wallet, I was so nervous I couldn't find it at first.

When I finally handed it over, the policeman looked at it carefully and noted that it was a brand new license.

He asked, "Don't you know you shouldn't back out into a main street?"

I couldn't bring myself to say, "Yes sir, I know but my daddy insisted that I do so."

Instead, I said, "Sir, yes sir and I will never do it again."

To my great relief, he said, "I'll let you go this time but if I ever hear about you doing something so dangerous and illegal again, I will come find you and take you downtown."

Nobody wanted to "go downtown" because that is where the jail was. I promised the policeman that I would obey the laws hereafter.

I drove around the block, essentially making a U-turn, and continued on to the lake.

Neither my father nor I said one word about what had just happened, but I can assure you that in later years when I was older, I teased him about it. We laughed many times about his causing me to be stopped the day after I got my license – busted by the cops for backing out into a main street.

Almost the Valedictorian

The "good little Gest boy" always earned good grades in school. I was continually on the honor roll and I even harbored hopes that I might be the class valedictorian.

This all changed in eleventh grade when I was only thirteen. I had skipped a few grades and so I was younger than anyone else in the class. They had pretty much gone through puberty and I was just starting.

My problem began in Industrial Arts, where we learned how to work with our hands. We made small wood projects, learning to use various tools like wrenches and hammers. And we learned how to grow plants, too. I liked the class and I remember with great satisfaction making a corner shelf. I sanded it to perfection and lacquered it with great care. When I took it home and presented it to my mother, she proudly displayed it so that anyone who visited could see my handiwork.

All was well until one the day the Industrial Arts teacher, Mr. Joe Steven, needed a wheelbarrow, and said, "Gest, go get us a wheelbarrow from the shed."

Instead of simply doing as I was told, I said, "If you want a wheelbarrow, you had better go get it yourself."

Not only was this uncharacteristic of me and surprising to everyone, I myself had no idea why or how those words shot out of my mouth.

"Well young man, you have just gotten yourself an "F" in this class."

That was it, over and done, an "F," despite my lovely corner shelf and my reputation as the good Gest boy; he was giving me an "F." I was afraid that my hopes of being first in the class might be over because of one smart-alecky sentence.

I was mortified. Even more so because I knew I was in big trouble at home.

Sure enough, when my mother heard about it, she told me how disappointed she was---in the form of lectures---for days.

And as I feared, the "F" lowered my grade point average (GPA). As a result, Martha Taylor was honored with the status of being our class valedictorian while I had to settle for salutatorian. I was only thirteen and already an "almost valedictorian."

After that, I learned to think before speaking, to not let whatever was rattling around in my brain go straight out my mouth.

Mama tried to ease my pain and said, "Boy, you were probably just suffering from a bad outbreak of testosterone." Most likely she added, "'you just smellin' yourself.' "

It was a common expression for telling you that you had gotten too big for your britches and that you were trying too hard to be a grown-up man. There have been other "almosts" in my life, but my "almost a Valedictorian" was the most painful.

49 Cents a Pound

The mathematics teacher at my school, Mr. Joseph T. Bivins, was one of my favorite teachers and more than a little eccentric. Some of us really thought the man was crazy at times. Later, it was my conclusion that he was crazy like a fox.

He even looked a little like a fox; five feet five inches tall, medium build, bald head, thin mustache, dark-skinned and strong as an ox. None of the other male teachers gave Mr. Bivins any guff. After all, he was not only strong; he was, as they said, "crazy."

Most of our teachers lived in town; Mr. Bivins lived 25 miles from Haines City. Other teachers dressed in what could be called "teacher garb." They wore ties, nice trousers or dresses, etc. It seemed Mr. Bivins wore whatever he laid his hands on when he reached into his closet. He drove an old, dirty beat-up Ford while most teachers drove late model cars that were usually clean and polished.

Most memorable of all was his tendency to challenge his students by using what we called outlandish and unheard of teaching methodologies. He was the only teacher who thought nothing of giving his students two hundred pages of overnight reading to do. And, then the next morning he would have us question each other on the reading assignment until he was satisfied that we understood what we had read.

These differences plus some things we heard he did and said in teacher faculty meetings cemented his reputation as being "different."

We just called him Crazy Joe Bivins. I will also say we loved him!

He pushed us hard and did his best to convince all of us that we could be whatever we wanted to be. His ability to explain complicated Math concepts was uncanny. I, who have never been very good at Math, understood most of the time.

I can still hear him repeating to me, "Gest, the area of a triangle is one-half times the base times the height – and don't you forget it."

Perhaps my most memorable experience with Mr. Bivins occurred one Spring morning when he rushed into class, nearly late. I say "nearly late" because in addition to being a great teacher, he was almost obsessive about doing things right and doing them right the first time. This, of course, included being on time and on schedule.

On this fine day, we were somewhat behind where he had expected us to be in working through the textbook. So, he apparently took advantage of his having to rush to get to class and the way he did it was to make a joke, which for him may not have been a joke. Therefore, we were not surprised when this tough old bird, said to us, his third period class, "I wish I had not been running late. As I passed through town, I looked over at the glass window of the A&P Super Market and guess what I saw? I saw a huge sign advertising brains for 49 cents a pound. Although I surmised these were pig brains, I nearly stopped anyway to buy some. Why? Because I reasoned that even if they were pig brains, they would probably be of immense help to the members of this class."

We were so stunned, we did not laugh at first. Mr. Bivins was no nonsense and usually nothing said by him in class was funny. However, after we recovered and thought about it, some of us broke out into gales of laughter. We talked about that day for many years after and this became just one of the legends of Mr. Joseph T. Bivins, one of the all-time great teachers of Mathematics.

There is little doubt in my mind that it was because of him and a few others on the teaching staff of Oakland High School that I managed to achieve what I have during my lifetime. So, thanks Mr. Bivins, as you roam around up there in Heaven, no doubt giving everyone there a hard time and all the while, holding them to a very high standard.

Conclusion

The mini-stories you have read are but a small sample of the many experiences which served to shape and mold me into the person I have become. They all tell the story of a young child who grew up in a deeply segregated community where every adult was a potential parent figure. Each adult felt it was her or his responsibility to make sure the young ones were respectful, courteous and well-behaved. To this day, I refer to older adults or those in positions of authority as "sir" or "ma'am".

I realize how trite it is and how common it may be to say it takes a village to raise a child. However, I firmly believe that if we as a Nation of Parents and Grandparents had not gotten away from that philosophy or mindset, our children would be much less likely to find themselves in detention facilities or other very difficult circumstances.

I hope those who read these short vignettes are taken back to those "olden days". It never hurts to look back and reflect on how and what our ancestors lived.